TRUST

D1602343

Abner Suarez

What Other Leaders Are Saying...

This book is a timely and compelling call to a lifestyle of faith in God. Abner wonderfully dissects Biblical examples to bring out what faith is, how God intends us to operate in it, and why. Abner does an excellent job of reminding us that, with God as our source and Jesus as our example, and we are Kingdom citizens with the responsibility and enablement to reign in life. *Trust: God's Unseen Power to Change the World* has within its pages the power to renew you and inspire you to believe as never before!

Our faith is the victory that overcomes the world! 1 John 5:4

DR. JERRY SAVELLE, INTERNATIONAL SPEAKER AND AUTHOR, CROWLEY, TX

AUTHOR OF BEST SELLERS: *IF SATAN CAN'T STEAL YOUR JOY,*
HE CAN'T KEEP YOUR GOODS AND *CALLED TO BATTLE, DESTINED TO WIN.*

WWW.JERRYSAVELLE.ORG

Abner Suarez has been a friend for many years. This book is not just a study in the subject of trust, but about his personal walk with God. I have personally seen him walk before God with total trust and bear much fruit in difficult and challenging situations. This book will help you understand the significance of trust in your relationship with God. It will also help you develop a deeper trust that will produce the fruit of heaven in the earth. Enjoy the adventure that all will experience that trust God.

APOSTLE DALE L. MAST, DESTINY CHRISTIAN CHURCH, DOVER, DE

AUTHOR: *AND DAVID PERCEIVED HE WAS KING, TWO SONS AND A FATHER,*
THE THRONE OF DAVID, SHATTERING THE LIMITATIONS OF PAIN

WWW.DESTINYDOVER.ORG

As a pastor for over 40 years, I've been asked one particular question constantly and consistently, how do I know that I'm really trusting God to answer my prayers and is my faith rooted in trusting Him? This book will show you how to trust God and build a life of walking in that trust. It will take you into a realm of faith that will propel you into doing great exploits for the Kingdom of God.

PASTOR AL BRICE, COVENANT LOVE CHURCH, FAYETTEVILLE, NC

WWW.MYCL.CHURCH

I have known Abner Suarez for many years. He has ministered to many people in various countries. His book, *Trust - God's unseen power to change the world*, has powerful insights and stories. He has a healing gift from God and is a man of integrity. I recommend him and his ministry.

DR. RANDY CLARK, MECHANICSBURG, PA

OVERSEER OF THE APOSTOLIC NETWORK OF GLOBAL AWAKENING

PRESIDENT OF GLOBAL AWAKENING THEOLOGICAL SEMINARY

WWW.GLOBALAWAKENING.COM

This book by my dear friend Abner Suarez will open your eyes once again to see what real God-faith looks like. This book will help us to captivate what we missed in the past when it comes to faith. I love the fresh revelation of faith, something I thought I knew all about until I read this manuscript. Today's walk is yesterday's faith-decree and to-day's faith-decree is tomorrow's walk. Faith will show in your walk, and your faith-walk will position you into places your best friends can never get you into. Release faith today from the inner-prison of self and prepare for a God-explosion in the natural. Do you desire to walk in a new dynamic? Make sure you read this book. I salute you, Abner Suarez!

ANDRE VAN ZYL

AUTHOR AND INTERNATIONAL SPEAKER, GOOD NEWS TO THE NATIONS, INC.

PRESIDENT: GLOBAL PRAYER ALLIANCE, DACULA, GA

WWW.GNNI.ORG

Abner is a remarkable man of God. He writes like he preaches, with conviction and a prophetic edge. He lives his message. He trusts God radically. One can't help but be drawn to trust in God in the same way as you read this book. As he notes, the hour of God's kingdom advance through faith-filled followers is upon us. The reader is drawn into deeper trust, rest, and focus on the purposes of the Lord. This is sorely needed in this hour of concurrent shaking and revival. Read, absorb, and be stirred!!

Dr. Peter Young, Bridgeway Church, Denver, CO

WWW.BRIDGEWAY.US

And in these end of days, before Yeshua returns, we will need a super-natural love and supernatural faith more than in any others. Yet most of the time, both of these spiritual attributes don't just materialize in us; they need to be walked out, experienced, and learned. I have known Abner Suarez personally for many years, and I can tell you that he lives what he says. In his latest book, you will learn from the ground up, firsthand from Abner's own experiences and powerful lessons of faith that can be applied to our day to day lives. This book is a must-read for all of us needing to build this faith and trust in God. Thank you, Abner!

Grant Berry, Founder, President Reconnecting Ministries

Author of Romans 911 - Time to Sound the Alarm!

WWW.RECONNECTINGMINISTRIES.ORG

It's my honor to recommend Abner's newest book. It is well written with an emphasis upon the true knowledge of God based on this one great truth: His Word is trustworthy. Our trust is in His written Word, both as Logos and Rhema. It is the foundation of what propels our faith into action.

The book is an instruction manual that will guide the readers into a closer intimate relationship with God and His purpose for their lives. It is truly a "pearl of great price" revealing that God and His Word are one. As the Apostle Paul declared to the Corinthians, "All of God's promises are yes in Jesus." Abner skillfully unpacks the Scriptures so that you will also agree with Paul with a resounding "Yes and Amen!"

Pastor Douglas Johnson

Pastor of Emeritus, Harvest Church, Hampstead, MD

Founder of Revealing the Father Ministries

TRUST

GOD'S UNSEEN POWER
TO CHANGE THE WORLD

Abner Suarez

HIGHERLIFE
PUBLISHING & MARKETING
Oviedo, FL

HigherLife Publishing & Marketing
  PO Box 623307
  Oviedo, FL 32762
  AHigherLife.com

Trust: God's Unseen Power to Change the World / Abner Suarez
  ISBN 978-1-951492-38-0 Paperback
  ISBN 978-1-951492-39-7 eBook
  ISBN 978-1-951492-73-1 Audiobook
  LOC # 1-10067270241

Printed in the United States of America
10 9 8 7 6 5 4 3 2 1

Contents

Dedication

I dedicate this book to my grandfather, Julio Lopez Pena, who pioneered a path for me and an entire generation of ministers that will come in our family line. With God's help, I will serve His purposes for my generation and pass the baton to the next.

> *And all these, having obtained a good testimony through faith, did not receive the promise, God having provided something better for us, that they should not be made perfect apart from us.* (Hebrews 11:39-40)

Acknowledgments

THE IDEA FOR THIS book was initially suggested to me by Pastor Al Brice. Pastor Al, thank you! The book is a little longer then you initially suggested, but I do believe it expresses the heart of God for this project. Your obedience has transformed my family's life for generations to come! You are a true shepherd and spiritual father. It as an honor to have you serve on our board of directors. I have watched and seek to follow your example of integrity and continual pursuit of friendship with God. Thank you for loving me and being a friend of God.

To my parents, Angel and Sara Suarez: Each day I seek to be an imitator of Jesus. Your prayers and labor from the time I was conceived to this day have not been in vain. With God's help, I will finish well.

To the entire ministry board of For Such A Time As This: One of the ways in which the blessings of the Lord have manifested in my life is through the covenant relationships you have with me; your unwavering love and support is invaluable. Thank you, Doug Johnson, Dale and LuAnne Mast, Mike and Debbie Sirianni, Grant Berry.

Melissa Wagner Pallotta, you have loved and cared for me as a member of your family and taken the vision God has given me as your own. Your prayers on my behalf have transformed thousands of individuals and churches. What you have sown in intercession will reap more than you could have imagined. Your greatest years of encounter and friendship with God are still ahead. May the Deborah anointing on your life be accelerated as never before and may your testimony be that God has truly been kind and faithful to me!

To every intercessor who is part of our prayer shield: Thank you for helping birth that which has been assigned to this ministry. This book is the fruit of your prayers. Perhaps we will live, never fully knowing that which your prayers, intercession, and declarations birthed for eternity. I so look forward to continually growing and continually expanding with you as a group in the coming season.

To every partner of For Such A Time As This: Thank you once again for being the foundation of the vision God has placed on my heart. Together with God's help, we will fufill our assignment in equipping reformers to display the brillance of God and disciple nations.

David Welday, meeting you nearly six years ago has been life-changing. You have caused me to see myself as God sees me. My life's work and ministry has been advanced through your support, encouragement, and advice. Thank you for taking every project we have worked on together as your own. You are a gift from God to me and a true friend.

Ellen M. King, thank you for partnering with me on this project. I believe your feedback, edits, and suggestions have allowed this project to be everything God desired it to be!

Chris W. Ritchie, Paul Metcalf, Donna Key, Ruth Mangiacapre, your love and friendship has shaped me into becoming that which God intended. Thank you!

Introduction

PEOPLE FROM ALL WALKS of life were constantly drawn to Him. He stood in stark contrast to the religious leaders of His day. He spoke words of life that carried an authority that caused the hearts of all who heard Him to be moved to a place of decision. Humanity had never seen a man do the miracles He had done on such a consistent basis. He came proclaiming that He was a King and preached the message of that kingdom. The kingdom He proclaimed did not fit any of the social or political movements of its day. John writes this at the close of his gospel:

> *And there are also many other things that Jesus did,*
> *which if they were written one by one, I suppose that*
> *even the world itself could not contain the books that*
> *would be written.*
> (John 21:25)

The Bible describes the written record God gave humanity, but that record most certainly cannot contain God. World history has been shaped forever by Jesus' birth, ministry, death, and resurrection.

One day, He was asked a most astonishing question:

> *"What shall we do, that we may work the works of*
> *God?" Jesus answered and said to them, "This is the*
> *work of God, that you believe in Him whom He sent."*
> (John 6:28-29)

I believe this question is remarkable on at least two different levels. The first is that those who asked the question believed it was possible to do the works of God as they were modeled in Jesus' life. Secondly, in His response, Jesus did not challenge the premise of the question, but instead gave a simple answer that could be easily understood and applied.

It is possible for humanity to do the works of God on earth. This is a truth that has shaped my life for the last twenty-five years. When I think about that, I often dream of what the earth would look like if even thirty percent of the world did the works of God. We can conclude from the totality of Scripture that it is God's will that all of humanity *can* do the works of God. If that happened, the earth would become what God desired from the beginning of time. We would live as God created us to live. The works of God could be accomplished if everyone chose to place their belief in Him.

The terms "faith" and "trust" are used interchangeably in this book.

The word "believe" is the Greek word *pisteuō* (used above in John 6:29) and defined as "to believe, trust, and put faith in."[1] Jesus' use of the word in this context and in this interaction also points to a central theme of the entire Bible: *trust in God.* It is God's invitation to humanity to place their faith in Him. Both the Old and the New Testaments view faith as mankind's trust in God.[2]

The Greek translation of the Old Testament, the Septuagint, employs the Greek *pistis* to translate several Hebrew words.[3] In the New Testament, the Greek noun *pistis* and the verb *pisteuō* both occur more than 240 times, while the adjective *pistos* is found 67 times.[4] It is, therefore, not a distortion of Jesus' answer to rephrase it in this

1.   James Strong, "4100. Pisteuó," Strong's Greek: 4100. Πιστεύω (pisteuó) – to believe, entrust (Biblehub), accessed May 13, 2020, https://biblehub.com/greek/4100.htm.

2.   A. C. Myers, *The Eerdmans Bible Dictionary* (Grand Rapids, MI: Eerdmans, 1987) 374.

3.   N. K. Gupta, "Faith" in J. D. Barry, et al., eds., *The Lexham Bible Dictionary* (Bellingham, WA: Lexham Press, 2016).

4.   L. L. Morris, "Faith" in D. R. W. Wood, et al., eds., *New Bible Dictionary* (Downers Grove, IL: InterVarsity Press, 1996) 358.

manner: "This is the work of God, that you trust (*pisteuō*) in Him whom He sent" (John 6:29).

Because they are two definitions of the word *pisteuō,* the terms "faith" and "trust" are used interchangeably in this book. Our trust and our confidence is placed in someone or something. That choice defines us and shapes our lives. What we trust compels us to choose one direction or task over another. We were created to trust God; when we do, we walk in peace and our faith (trust) grows even deeper through our experiences with Him.

I purchased a new vehicle about three years ago. My trust in the company that manufactured it was one of the overiding factors that propelled me to make the purchase. I knew they produced well-made vehicles through my own experience and by their reputation. I also had confidence that if it malfunctioned, the company would honor the warranty that came with the purchase. For nearly nineteen years, I have been flying on one particular airline and its partners around the world. I trust that when I purchase a ticket, they will competently bring me to my desired destination. The trust I have in this airline is based on the overwhelmingly positive experience I have had as a customer and a frequent flier.

Nations are also defined by the trust (or lack of trust) their citizens have for them. This is usually based on the form of government that is in control. Many dictators initially assumed power in a democratic manner because they promised a reality that was appealing to the masses at that time. Hitler did this. *He was elected.* He did not take over Germany by force. There are many other examples, but the point is this: *That which we trust defines our world.* All of humanity (born-again or not) is defined by their internal belief system that chooses to trust certain realities and truths.

When humanity trusts God in the correct manner, we abide in Him and replicate His works here on earth. The gospel writers consistently agreed on this. Jesus' emphasis in His teaching on trust was the key to walking in the life God desires for all of humanity. Here are some examples:

And these signs will follow those who believe [trust]: In My name they will cast out demons; they will speak with new tongues; they will take up serpents; and if they drink anything deadly, it will by no means hurt them; they will lay hands on the sick, and they will recover. (Mark 16:17-18, addition mine)

Jesus said to her, "Did I not say to you that if you would [trust] believe you would see the glory of God?" (John 11:40, addition mine)

So Jesus answered and said to them, "Have faith [trust] in God." (Mark 11:22, addition mine)

"Most assuredly, I say to you, he who [trusts] believes in Me, the works that I do he will do also; and greater works than these he will do, because I go to My Father." (John 14:12, addition mine)

In each of these verses, the word translated "believe" is the same word that means "to trust." Our simple choice to trust God is a gift from Him. Through it, we can shape the world according to God's divine design! Trust, though unseen, is a substance that can shape every part of our lives. God has never created anyone without first making provision for them in every way. Our trust in God opens the windows of heaven over our lives and allows God's abundant provision to be made a reality. Our trust in God allows us to see and understand reality from God's perspective. Our trust in God will allow us to reshape our family's history according to His intent. However, trust in God does not guarantee a life without trouble or difficulty; it's actually the reverse. There is

Jesus' emphasis in His teaching on trust was the key to walking in the life God desires for all of us.

a biblical guarantee that if we live a life of trust in God, we will be persecuted. So why do it? Simple. Trusting God ushers us into the life we were meant to enjoy and the only one in which we can reach our potential, fulfill our calling, and find the deepest possible level of personal satisfaction all at the same time.

We are invited to the beauty of a life that not only replicates Jesus' life and ministry but also displays even greater works in the earth through the abilities He has placed within us.[5] However, what God *intends* for humanity and what we *actually experience* are often two separate realities. The deficit is never on God's end. Perhaps you have experienced this. You know what God has promised in Scripture but have never experienced that truth as a reality. Or maybe you have never considered that through simple trust in God, your life could be shaped according to God's divine design. Perhaps you have experienced a measure of the promises of God but are longing to see the provision of God's promises to a deeper extent. Or maybe you are just beginning this journey of trusting God as a lifestyle.

> **Trust, though unseen, is a substance that can shape every part of our lives.**

Regardless of your current life experience, this book was created to challenge, inspire, and equip you to live a lifestyle of trusting God, according to God's divine design. As you make the choice to trust God, you will, indeed, see the words of Jesus manifested in your life. You will do the works of God! If you are in Christ, God is completely committed to seeing His purpose for eternity established in your life. God's plan for you is simple: Trust in Him. This simple choice to trust in Him will produce a life of victory and hope, not just for you, but for you and your entire family!

This book is a tool to help you form a biblical worldview, and enable you, through the power of the Holy Spirit, to build your life on the solid foundation of steadfast trust in God. It is certainly not an exhaustive writing on the subject of faith; but as you read, you will find that living a lifestyle of faith as God intended involves embracing multiple biblical values and mindsets. Therefore, a lifestyle of faith is of a synergistic nature.

---

5.   See John 14:12.

Living a lifestyle of faith can be likened to the way the human body was created to function. The human body consists of a number of biological systems that carry out specific functions; each are necessary for everyday optimal living. If any of these systems are not functioning properly, our body will not function to its fullest potential.

The call to live a lifestyle of faith is simplistic, but it also necessitates that we embrace multiple core values. Therefore, you will find that certain truths are emphasized repeatedly using different language or a slightly different lens. This is intentional for two reasons, the first being that it follows Paul's apostolic instruction that "faith comes by hearing, and hearing by the word of God" (Romans 10:17). In our current setting, we can declare that faith comes by *reading*.

Secondly, I have learned from experience that if we are to trust God properly, we must think properly. To think properly, we must be delivered of any incorrect and demonic thought processes we have embraced. In the journey to think properly, I have learned that I must hear truth *again and again and again!* Amos prophesied that there would be "a famine on the

If you are in Christ, God is completely committed to seeing His purpose for eternity established in your life.

land, not a famine of bread, nor a thirst for water, but of hearing the words of the Lord" (Amos 8:11). My prayer for you is that you would have a continual ear to hear words from the Lord. A people who live a lifestyle of faith love to continually hear the Lord.

I have opened each chapter with the Word of God followed by a word from the Lord for this current season in obedience to a command from the Holy Spirit. Peter admonishes us in his epistle that we might be "established in the present truth" to "make your call and election sure" (2 Peter 1:10, 12). The Word of the Lord allows us to make our calling and election sure, but it is also vital to live a lifestyle of faith. I believe the words I have included are straight from the heart of God and applicable for this current time. This is a season of pioneers. God is in need of pioneers because His greatest desire and purposes have yet to be fulfilled. He is revealing truth for those who have ears to hear. God is in need of people whose level of faith rises to His level and desire. Pioneers will be raised up, both men and women, to not only hear, but *believe,* the truth. As they believe the "truth," a new renaissance will be birthed in the body of Christ that will shape world history in a manner we have never seen before.

As I complete this manuscript, nations worldwide are facing a global pandemic called COVID-19. The truths contained here, which I believe are firmly rooted in Scripture, are always relevant and applicable. One of the beauties of God's Word and His kingdom is that the manner in which it functions and operates never changes. The principles

> **Pioneers will be raised up, both men and women, to not only hear, but *believe*, the truth.**

in this book can be applied by any person, regardless of gender, ethnicity, culture, or economic status. It will enable them to live their life in the manner God created them to live.

Last of all, I want to encourage you to be like the Bereans. They:

> *Received the word with all readiness, and searched the Scriptures daily to find out whether these things were so.*
> (Acts 17:11)

Take the time to consider all teaching according to the full counsel of God. I esteem both those who are hungry to receive my message, as well as those who may be reluctant about its content. I encourage both parties to search these truths for themselves.

Nearly twenty-four years ago, I began my personal journey of endeavoring to trust God with my whole life. The entire trajectory of my life changed in one moment of intentional surrender. From that time on, I knew I was called as a minister of the gospel. I knew that one day I would go around the world preaching the gospel and that God would allow me to see an unprecedented move of God in my generation. Up to that moment in my life, I had never desired to be in ministry nor had I ever considered it as part of my purpose, even remotely. Sincere and intentional surrender unlocked God's purpose for my life. I began to understand surrender and how placing my complete trust in God opens His unlimited possibilities to us.

While I had now discovered part of my purpose, the circumstances of my life did not change immediately simply because God had given me an understanding of that purpose. God was inviting me on an eternal journey of trusting Him. As I endeavored to trust Him, my life began to be shaped according to His divine design. While I have certainly made many mistakes and taken some wrong turns along the way, God has been faithful to

> **Living a lifestyle of faith is not a destination, but a journey.**

fulfill His Word. My life is a living testimony to God's goodness. He has allowed me the privilege of ministering the gospel of the kingdom in twenty-three nations. My eyes have seen what I had never conceived in my wildest imagination: The lame have walked, the blind see, the bound have been set free, and the good news of the kingdom of God has been preached!

I freely admit that I am not a finished product; in fact, the only wisdom I can claim is what God has given me as a gift. I, like you, am on an eternal journey, seeking to love God with all my heart and love His people as He would.

Seeing God's goodness in my life has not been the result of my own talent or gifting. No, it stems from learning to use God's faith to receive what He has already prepared for me before the foundation of the world. I am still learning to live and walk by God's faith daily. Living a lifestyle of faith is not a destination, but a journey. It is a journey in which we constantly grow and continually learn.

Throughout this book, I use the term, "God's divine design." It is simply my description of God's purpose and intent in creating the world and mankind. "*Divine* is defined as proceeding directly from God."[6] Design is defined as "a particular purpose and intention held

---

6. "Divine," Merriam-Webster (Merriam-Webster), accessed May 25, 2020, https://www.merriam-webster.com/dictionary/divine)

by an individual."[7] In this case, we are talking about God's design. It is of the utmost importance that we intimately understand His original intent and divine design for the earth. His intent was established when time began, and the manner in which He desires to relate to humanity has never changed. And it never will.

"For I am Lord, I do not change."   (Malachi 3:6)

Abner Suarez

May 2020

---

7.   "Design," Merriam-Webster (Merriam-Webster), accessed May 25, 2020, https://www.merriam-webster.com/dictionary/design)

CHAPTER I

God's Original Intent

In the beginning God created...
(Genesis 1:1 NIV)

April 6, 2020
Words from Heaven

SINCE THE BEGINNING OF *time I have longed for this season. I have truly allowed everything that can be shaken to be shaken, and I am causing My people to live from a secure foundation as never before. Over the coming season, I will give wisdom, knowledge, and understanding on how to build an even deeper and stronger foundation to My people, and I will release an unprecedented move of My Spirit in the earth in this time. I will pour out My Spirit in the nations of the earth as I never have before, and there will be a clear differentiation between true and false within My people in this season. I will cause My light to shine through My people as never before and I will cause darkness that has rooted itself around the globe and in certain nations to be displaced with kingdom realities.*

My people must position themselves correctly in this hour, for this is truly a season of the restoration of all things. I am restoring My people to that which I originally intended. This is a season in which I desire to release wisdom to govern and have authority in the specific place and purpose for which I have called each of them. This is indeed a unique season in the earth—one in which I am opening heaven and opening My people's eyes to see what no other generation of My children has seen; but know this: With the ability to see comes great responsibility in the areas of stewardship and correct and proper behavior.

The Bible is an indescribable gift from God to mankind. In it, we find the ability to know God, our origins in God, a blueprint for building nations, and a tool for each believer to receive victory in every area of life. We're meant to understand the Bible and have fellowship with the God who wrote it. The Word of God must be understood through the full counsel of Scripture from Genesis to Revelation. The same God who showed His faithfulness and lovingkindness to His people in the Old Testament set the stage for the extraordinary revelation of Himself in Jesus in the New Testament. He's the same God in both places; we need to come to know Him through *both*.

God was intentionally teaching His people how to do the same and how much God-power is released when His Word is declared.

In the very first book of the Bible, Genesis, God reveals Himself as a God who operates in patterns. What was the first one? Speech! God spoke. God created the earth to be governed by words. As He spoke, the ideas that filled His mind came into being. God literally and simply verbalized everything that came into existence. He carefully arranged His creation process through the words of His mouth. He began with light. Then came the earth and the seas, the moon and the sun, and then living things. Five of His creative acts had the ability to reproduce themselves: plants, fish, birds, animals, and mankind. In choosing this method and then recording it for posterity, God was intentionally teaching His people how to do the same and how much God-power is released when His Word is declared.

As God spoke, the earth responded to His voice.

God spoke: "Light!" And light appeared.
(Genesis 1:3 MSG)

He commanded the earth and it separated into land and seas, and later was filled with plants and trees; and He pronounced that it was good. He placed the sun and the moon in their places (after the light)! Then He spoke again, forming birds, fish, animals, and finally, us.

Mankind was the chief object of God's affection and the only one *made like Him*. No other aspect of creation was made in the image of God. Dr. Pauline Walley-Daniels writes, "Humanity was given an aspect of God's personality."[8] The Bible says:

> *Then God said, "Let Us make man in Our image, according to Our likeness; let them have dominion over the fish of the sea, over the birds of the air, and over the cattle, over all the earth and over every creeping thing that creeps on the earth." So God created man in His own image; in the image of God He created him; male and female He created them. Then God blessed them, and God said to them, "Be fruitful and multiply; fill the earth and subdue it; have dominion over the fish of the sea, over the birds of the air, and over every living thing that moves on the earth."* (Genesis 1:26-28)

After He made mankind, He did not say it was good: He said it was *very* good!

The first human beings were created to relate to God in a very specific manner. They were created perfect and without flaw, and placed into perfect paradise. From the beginning, they were created to know God's approval without ever having to perform

God's voice was the first sound they ever heard.

for Him in any manner.[9] From a posture of complete approval, they were to spend eternity knowing the God who could never be exhausted. God created Adam and Eve to be dependent solely on Him; they weren't supposed to ever take care of themselves. They were created

---

8. Pauline Walley-Daniels, PhD., *The Holy Spirit: the Power of the Spoken Word* (Denver, CO: Outskirts Press, 2015).
9. See Genesis 1:31.

to have complete trust in God as the Source for everything they would ever need. Adam and Eve could find all they required, either in God or in the paradise in which God had placed them.[10] God desired to establish His kingdom on the earth as it existed in heaven through a family called humanity for eternity. God's primary interest was the establishment of His kingdom on the earth, not a religion called Christianity. Trust was an essential element of the way Adam and Eve were to relate to God. The perfect Creator could be trusted in every way.

Mankind had been made male and female in God's own image. Just as the plants, trees, and animals had the ability to reproduce and were commanded to be fruitful and multiply, so were Adam and Eve; however, God also gave them something else: dominion. They had dominion over all the earth. God told them to "fill the earth and subdue it." After He created them, the first thing God did was *speak* to them. God's voice was the first sound they ever heard. God's voice commissioned and qualified Adam and Eve to govern the earth.[11] Kenneth Copeland once said that we are supposed to "be owners of the earth with stewardship responsibilities." In commissioning Adam and Eve, God established a principle on the way He desired to relate to all of humanity—through His voice. The voice that set the universe in order as God intended, was also to guide humanity as God intended.

God will not violate His own word.

When God gave humanity the creation He had just made, *He meant it.* When He did this, God made a willful choice over how He would relate to His own creation *for eternity*. God put the earth under mankind's governance and authority. God intended that they would govern the earth *in partnership with Him*. God made the sovereign choice to express His will for the earth through the faith humanity placed in Him, and the knowledge He communicated to them through the words He spoke. Once God uttered that mandate and put it in motion, He would never go back on it. He will not violate His own word. It's in stone and will never be repealed by Him.

---

10.   See Genesis 1:29.
11.   See Psalm 8:6.

Adam and Eve were also given the gift of choice. The choices that Adam and Eve made many thousands of years ago still govern the current state of our planet.

Adam and Eve were given God's blessing to have dominion, favor, and authority over all creation. Their first act of co-laboring with God was the naming of the animals.[12] Adam named the animals by speaking God's words, just as God had modeled when He created the earth. This narrative presents a unique insight into how God intended to relate to us. God is the Source. He brought the animals to Adam. Just as God's words set the universe into motion, Adam's voice became God's voice, and the animals were set into the order God intended. What is fascinating is that Adam does not ask God to name the animals; he simply releases the Word of God over the animals. The same creative gift God had was extended and given as a gift to all of mankind. The brilliant and perfect mind Adam was given at creation as well as God's mandate over them, giving them dominion "over all the earth" qualified Adam to name the animals as God intended.

Humanity's trust in God's words was the essential bridge that connected man to God's purpose and His will. The words God spoke to humanity and mankind's faith in those words were the avenue by which Adam and Eve could function in the powerful position of dominion over the earth that they were given. Humanity must place their trust in God's words and act upon the power that God releases in His Word: This is foundational for establishing God's will on the earth. Adam and Eve's trust in God caused them to have God's view of the earth.

From the moment of their creation, Adam and Eve were fully equipped to accomplish the task of stewarding the world. They were intelligent and beautiful. By meeting with God in the cool of the day, God intended that His knowledge and wisdom would govern the world through the hearts of this couple and their offspring. As they listened to the voice of God, they were educated through that communication; man's spirit communed with God, and mankind reigned over the earth. Especially created for this position of authority, mankind had a great

---

12.   See Genesis 2:19-20.

responsibility. Their greatest pleasure in life was found in knowing God and operating in the purpose for which He had placed them here!

However, a change took place that forever altered God's original intent for humanity and the earth. Adam and Eve, who were commanded to "subdue" the earth, dialogued with the devil instead who appeared to them as a cunning serpent.[13] As a result of Adam and Eve's failure to subdue the earth, they came into agreement with the devil and the earth was forever changed. The devil now had legal right to the gift God had given to Adam and Eve: the earth.

The effects on Adam and Eve were immediately evident. This one act cost humanity their innocence and their ability to see reality from only God's perspective. Trust in satan's lie caused their vision of each other and God to become flawed. They saw each other as naked and in shame. They turned away from the God who came lovingly searching for them. Instead of drawing near to God as they should have, they were fearful. They were ashamed and they blamed each other.[14] They lost sight of their God-given identity.

The Babylonian system can be defined as man's way of trying to make it in this world without God.

The lens by which we perceive the world becomes distorted when the foundation of our life is not in trusting God. The lens through which Adam and Eve saw God and the reality of the world around them became fatally flawed. Believing words that are not God's word causes our life and the world around us to be distorted. We act on what we believe; therefore, our beliefs define our behavior. God created humanity to live with a belief system, and our belief system is shaped by the voice each person adopts as their foundation for their belief system. All of humanity is living by faith. The question is this: Who and what are we placing our faith in and how is that shaping our world?

Adam and Eve's fatal mistake ushered in a whole new paradigm in the earth. This agreement empowered the enemy, enabling him to

---

13.　See Genesis 3:1-7.

14.　See Genesis 3:7-13.

operate here. As a result, the Babylonian system, something God never intended, began operating. The Babylonian system can be defined as man's way of trying to make it in this world without God. At its very core, the Babylonian system teaches that mankind must depend on its own way, its own resources, its own efforts, and its own ideas to achieve success. The world system is designed to exert unrelenting pressure on every person, even after one achieves success. Success does not release us from its clutches.

A couple of years ago, I was channel surfing, and ran across a reality television program. The program followed the life of a successful young man who ran a real estate firm in New York City. The young man was about to be married and he was running ragged. He was not helping with the wedding preparations because of his grueling work schedule. His fiancé wanted help. In a heated response, the young man explained to his fiancé that as the boss, he had employees who depended on his performance for their livelihood. The young man, who was remarkably successful in the eyes of many, had embraced the classic lie of the Babylonian world system. He believed he was created to take care of himself. For thousands of years, humanity has continually tried to create philosophies and systems that would enable them to return once again to the perfect world that existed when time began. Each of them fail miserably because they are godless at the core.

The fall may have put the earth out of order, but it did nothing to upset God's original intent. Though humanity had forsaken its assignment in the earth, God did not forsake His commitment to humanity. Even before the world began, it had been decided that Jesus, who would come to earth as fully God and fully man, would die for the restoration of God's original plan for humanity and the earth He created.[15] Though the enemy had changed the course of how God intended the earth to operate, God immediately let His intentions be known to the devil:

---

15.   See Revelation 13:8.

"And I will put enmity between you and the woman, and between your seed and her Seed; He shall bruise your head, and you shall bruise His heel."   (Genesis 3:15)

God told the devil that He would ultimately redeem humanity and regain ownership of the earth once again. Not only would God win, but He would do it through the offspring of a woman, a descendant of Eve, whom the enemy had deceived. Man could and would be redeemed—despite the poor choices of Adam and Eve!

Key Concepts from Chapter 1

- God's divine design from the beginning of time has not changed.

- Humanity was created to be completely dependent upon God, so they would choose to trust Him as the Source of all they would ever need for eternity.

- Humanity was created for the specific purpose of being a steward of the earth.

- Humanity was created to be educated and governed by knowledge that came from listening to the voice of God.

- Humanity's choice to trust and act upon the wrong voice changed them and the earth forever.

CHAPTER 2

Faith Originates with God

"Have God's faith."
(Mark 11:22 BBE)

April 6, 2020
Words from Heaven

WHEN I CHOSE TO *create a people made in My image, I created them to never be without. At their very core, I created them to find their deepest needs and satisfaction for their existence in Me. All that was Mine I intended to freely give to them. I gave them the earth that I created, and put within them the desire to build, establish, and dream with Me. I gave to them the methods I used to create the earth. As they trusted Me for eternity, My people were never to be without. From my lovingkindness, I longed to be the Source of My people's strength and the power behind them.*

Indeed, I say to My people today: This is a season in the earth in which the power of faith and the ability to speak to mountains that I never desired or ordained to exist on earth has come. The time has come for My people to walk and live and experience the power of My faith as never before. While even some of My very own children have disregarded and mocked the message of faith, this will be a seaon in which the true message of faith is preached, lived, and declared as never before. Did not My Son question whether or not He would find faith on earth when He returned? I desire that My people choose to trust, believe, and speak words of faith and words of life. Yes, this is a season in the earth for trusting and believing, Again, this is a season for trusting, believing and speaking words of life!

The Godhead's commitment to humanity began long before humans were created. Even though Adam and Eve had abdicated their legal authority to operate in the earth and given satan a foothold, God had already foreseen the poor choices His first created beings would make. Before the foundation of the world, the Godhead had planned that Jesus, God the Son, would come to earth and be conceived by God the Holy Spirit in a young virgin named Mary.[16]

God would give the gift of Himself to humanity, so that His original plan for humanity could be fulfilled. Jesus would come to earth as God, intentionally choosing to live within the limits of humanity.[17] Jesus came to earth as the second Adam.[18] By placing Himself under these limitations, Jesus modeled God's original intent for Adam. Jesus, the Son of Man, would have complete faith in the Father and the Holy Spirit. The power of Jesus' life and ministry rested upon His faith in the Father and the power of the Holy Spirit. Jesus did not come to earth with His own agenda; He came to fulfill the will of the Father.[19]

All that God desired for humanity would be displayed in the life and ministry of Jesus. The Bible leaves us a clear record. Jesus, as the second Adam, lived and fulfilled all God had planned for the first Adam. Jesus would live a completely sinless life.[20] He would overcome every temptation of the evil one.[21] Jesus was completely governed by the voice of God.[22] He was a living and breathing expression

---

16.   See Revelation 13:8, Luke 1:35.
17.   See Philippians 2:5-8.
18.   See 1 Corinthians 15:45.
19.   See John 6:38.
20.   See Isaiah 53:9; 1 Peter 2:22.
21.   See John 14:30.
22.   John 5:19.

of the Father-heart of God to humanity.[23] He came preaching and demonstrating the gospel of good news.[24] He healed all manner of sickness and disease because it was never God's intention for those evils to be part of man's existence in the first place.[25] Jesus was consumed with God's passion to redeem humanity and the earth. This was His divine mission. As the second Adam, He succeeded in reestablishing God's original plan so we could be free in Him.

One key distinction between Adam and Jesus was that in the garden at creation, God walked *with* Adam, but in Jesus, for the first time in human history, God lived *in* man. The temple of God was now literally living in man.[26] An essential element of the mission of Jesus was to preach and demonstrate the kingdom of God, but God's plan could not be fulfilled without Jesus' death and resurrection. Only through this divine

> **Jesus, as the second Adam, lived and fulfilled all God had planned for the first Adam.**

mission of death and resurrection could God's full desire for humanity be realized. For the joy set before Him, Jesus endured the cross, so that humanity might be redeemed to Himself.[27]

After His death and resurrection, Jesus gloriously appeared to His disciples. Just as God had breathed the breath of life into humanity, Jesus now breathed into His disciples that very same breath of life.[28] He charged them to make disciples of all nations, walking in the same authority He had.[29] (He could do this because He had regained mankind's authority when He redeemed us.) He also promised them that He would always be with them. He literally restored us to what He intended from the beginning of time.

23. See Colossians 1:15.
24. See Luke 4:18.
25. See Matthew 4:23.
26. See John 1:14.
27. See 1 Corinthians 15:20-23, Hebrews 12:2.
28. See Genesis 2:7, John 20:22.
29. See Matthew 28:16-20.

The first Adam was not created to take care of himself, and neither was this new race of people created to take care of themselves. For humanity to become "born-again," God Himself would give them the key that would unlock the door into a new identity and a new way of living. This new way of living was a reintroduction of what God desired at the beginning of time: a people who lived as citizens in His kingdom representing His interests in the earth. This kingdom (God's rule and reign) is what Jesus taught, modeled, and demonstrated fully in His life on earth. Humanity would no longer have to live under the disastrous effects of the Babylonian system. The key to unlocking this new identity and way of life is the gift of faith.

Through the life and ministry of Jesus, the Son of Man, God was reintroducing humanity to His original intention, a life built on a foundation of faith. In Mark's gospel, we find an account of Jesus finding a fig tree that had no figs because it was not the appropriate season. It should be noted that even though it was not the season for figs, there *should have been* fruit if there were leaves on that tree, as the fruit on a fig tree begins to grow *before* the leaves do. Jesus spoke to the tree, declaring: "Let no one eat fruit from you ever again" (Mark 11:14).The following morning, Peter was astonished because the words of Jesus had happened exactly as He had said. The tree was withered to its very roots.[30] Then Jesus gave His disciples a lesson on the subject of faith. He began the lesson by saying: "Have God's faith" (Mark 11:22, BBE). Jesus began with a startling revelation of God Himself: God has faith! Yes, God has faith, and He has made the type of faith He possesses and uses available to everyone. The key to the faith that God gives originates within God Himself.

Archibald Robertson, a renowned Greek scholar, explained it like this: "In Mark 11:22… we rightly translate 'have faith in God,'

> **It is God's revelation of Himself that is the basis of our faith in Him.**

---

30.   See Mark 11:20.

though the genitive [the Greek case] does not mean 'in,' but only the *God kind of faith.*[31] God gives all of us this "God kind of faith."

Faith is an ability which God possesses within Himself to achieve His divine purpose. Faith is God's enduring confidence in His own attributes to fulfill that which His mind and heart have deemed desirable and good.[32] The community of the Trinity known as the Father, Son, and Holy Spirit, though distinct persons, are one God in complete unity. Therefore, when the Godhead operates in faith, they achieve their desired result. Amazingly, this same confidence has been made available to all of us as well!

God has this faith within Himself and His own attributes. The faith God offers us has the power to take us out of ourselves and into complete dependence upon God. Faith is not simply an agreement or an intellectual acceptance that certain things are true. It is possible for me to believe that something exists but still never place my "faith" in that truth. People might agree that Jesus Christ walked this earth, taught like no other prophet, performed

> **Faith is a gift God gave humanity to release His ability to work on our behalf.**

miracles like no other man, and even died and rose from the dead on the third day, *but still never place their faith in that reality.*

It is God's revelation of Himself that is the basis of our faith in Him. A believer and citizen of the kingdom of God is one who responds by faith to God through trusting God's revelation of Himself found in Scripture as the basis of his or her existence. Jesus revealed Himself as the way, truth, and the life (to the human race).[33] God's love, His standards, and all His attributes are found in His Word and in the person of Jesus Christ.

---

31. Archibald T. Robertson, *A Grammar of the Greek New Testament in the Light of Historical Research* (Nashville, TN: Broadman, 1980).
32. See 1 Samuel 2:35.
33. See John 14:6.

When the good news of the gospel is presented to humanity, everyone is given a choice between life and death.[34] Adam and Eve, though created perfect and made to trust God in every way, were also given a choice; God continues to honor the choices of humanity today. We are all entrusted with a measure of faith to the gospel message.[35] God gives each of us the ability to respond to Him, but we must make the decision to say yes!

It is as though God asked us to run a marathon. He has already done all the training and given us everything we need to complete the course. All we have to do is show up for the race, trust Him, and draw on His strength to run. Empowered by God Himself to make the choice and run the marathon, we can win that race and enjoy an abundant life with Him.

Faith is a gift God gave humanity to release His ability to work on our behalf. Faith can only be received through complete surrender and trust. It cannot be earned through good works or performance. Faith in God precedes good works, and good works are the fruit of genuine faith; however, true faith is birthed by simple trust. The apostle Paul writes:

> *For by grace you have been saved through faith, and that not of yourselves; it is the gift of God, not of works, lest anyone should boast. For we are His workmanship, created in Christ Jesus for good works, which God prepared beforehand that we should walk in them.*
> (Ephesians 2:8-10)

Faith is the lens through which we interact with God. Kingdom living requires that we draw on it constantly as we go through our everyday lives.

---

34.   See Deuteronomy 30:19-20.
35.   See Romans 12:3.

Key Concepts from Chapter 2

- Jesus came as the Son of God and Son of Man but chose to live as the Son of Man.

- Jesus, as the Son of Man, expressed God's original intent for humanity.

- God has faith and God operates in faith.

- God offers faith as a gift to humanity.

- Humanity is given the power to choose to receive God's faith as a gift.

- Choosing to place our faith in God is not simply an intellectual agreement, but a choice to surrender our entire existence to God's purposes.

CHAPTER 3

God Gives Humanity Faith to Overcome the World

For whatever is born of God overcomes the world.
And this is the victory that has overcome the world—our faith.
(1 John 5:4)

April 6, 2020
Words from Heaven

I NEVER CREATED MEN or women to fail. I never intended that humanity live in distress or discomfort. I never created humanity to live with sickness, evil, or depression. I created them to live for eternity exploring My heart, My wisdom, and My gracious intentions toward them. My heart is grieved when humanity chooses to live below the power and the place that I have created for each of them. I created humanity to be a success in every way, that they would find their greatest satisfaction in Me. That they would know Me and love Me with all their heart and soul and mind.

I have a solution for every evil in this world—this is the season in which I want to release godly solutions to My people. In this season in the earth, I will put My people on display. My sons and daughters will display the unique distinction and power that is found in them when they walk in Me and enforce the victory I have given them for all humanity. In this time, the earth is shifting and changing according to My divine intent because I will have a people who display and live in victory in every area of life. A new sound of victory will come to the nations of the earth because I have ordained that families will walk in victory. Apostolic church communities will walk in victory, and the cities and regions of the earth will benefit because of the victory of my people. This is a time to draw close to Me, My people, so that you might see and experience the salvation power I have ordained for you, My people. Indeed, this is a divine season of victory, hope, and overcoming for My people in the earth.

We know that humanity was placed on earth to represent God as an ambassador of His kingdom when time began. An ambassador is a minister of the highest rank, employed by a prince or state, who lives at the court of another to manage the public concerns of his own prince or state, and represents the power and dignity of a sovereign.[36] As an ambassador of God, humanity was given complete ownership of the earth with the responsibility to define it according to God's divine design. Humanity was chosen exclusively by God to be stewards over the earth.

> *The Lord God made the earth and the heavens before any plant of the field was in the earth and before any herb of the field had grown. For the Lord had not caused it to rain on the earth, and there was no man to till the ground; but a mist went up from the earth and watered the whole face of the ground.* (Genesis 2:5-6)

Humanity was never to be defined by the earth or the circumstances of the earth. The earth was to be defined by the men and women who placed their complete trust in God.

Humanity was charged to advance and extend heaven on earth, so that the place God gave mankind to steward would be a replica of the

---

36. Noah Webster, "Ambassador" *1828 American Dictionary of the English Language*, original facsimile edition (Chesapeake, VA: Foundation for American Christian Education, 1968).

place God chose to dwell (heaven). God intended that earth would be a colony of heaven. Gold and onyx were part of the landscape:

> *And the gold of that land is good. Bdellium and onyx*
> *stone are there.*   (Genesis 2:12)

At that time, the earth was in a state of complete perfection. God's will for humanity was that they would live for eternity, knowing the pleasure and beauty of God and having the privilege of stewarding the earth which He created for their discovery and enjoyment. There was no strife, evil, sickness, or injustice. God never intended for humanity to experience pain, death, sickness, poverty, or any other evil that resulted from Adam's disobedience.

When Adam and Eve fell, the earth was shattered along with their minds and hearts. For thousands of years, man and the creation suffered together because of their sin. And then Jesus came. He preached and sacrificed Himself. Through His death, resurrection, and ascension, a door opened to humanity on earth for the goodness of the kingdom of God.

After Jesus completed His destiny, God's divine design for humanity could once again become a reality. The kingdom of God could now be established in the earth through humanity in the very same manner it had been established through the life of Jesus. God's words to Adam had been these:

> *"Be fruitful and multiply; fill the earth and subdue it;*
> *have dominion ove the fish of the sea, over the birds of*
> *the air, and over every living thing that moves on the*
> *earth."*   (Genesis 1:28)

God's design for humanity could now become a reality. Jesus came to earth and fulfilled His mission of restoring that which was lost.[37] His mission was to benefit all of humanity. In every culture and every nation, His fulfilled mission would be "good tidings of great joy which will be for all people" (Luke 2:10). Jesus did not come to complete

---

37.   See Luke 19:10.

the task of establishing and advancing the kingdom of God. Instead, He made it possible for men and women to fulfill their purpose in the manner God originally intended. The kingdom of God which Jesus so gloriously represented when He walked on the earth has now been conferred on all who choose to trust Him. Jesus declared this:

> *"And I bestow upon you a kingdom just as My Father bestowed one upon me."* (Luke 22:29)

Jesus lived a life of victory over the Babylonian system and His death and resurrection made victory possible for all of humanity in the here and now. Across the nations of the earth, we continue to see people experiencing the disastrous impact of original sin and the continuing consequences of the Babylonian system. Unjust systems rule nations around the planet. Millions of people whom God created to live an abundant life live under the tyranny and effects of the Babylonian system instead. Those who are in Christ are invited to live like Jesus. We are invited to live a life of complete victory over the Babylonian system and in turn, offer humanity an invitation into the abundant life the kingdom of God offers to all. We are invited to live out the truth Jesus declared in a parable: "Do business till I come" (Luke 19:13).

Heaven coming to earth was God's intention from the beginning of time.

When people see a believer, they should see an ambassador of God, who is fully able to proclaim and manifest the kingdom of God in every aspect of their lives.[38] God's kingdom is in need of representatives who believe that God will release an answer to the prayer Jesus taught His disciples to pray:

> *"Your kingdom come. Your will be done on earth as it is in heaven."* (Matthew 6:10)

Heaven coming to earth was God's intention from the beginning of time and it still is today. God's mandate and vision for His body is not

---

38. See 2 Corinthians 5:20.

simply to exist, but to forcefully bring His dominion into this present age. Because Jesus' successful mission forever changed history, God can now invite His body to corporately express His will *on earth as it is in heaven* and change human history according to His divine design.

Heaven coming to earth is only possible when God's people trust Him, so that this reality can be expressed. In the old covenant, God promised the nation of Israel this:

> *"Therefore you shall lay up these words of mine in your heart and in your soul, and bind them as a sign on your hand, and they shall be as frontlets between your eyes."*
> (Deuteronomy 11:18)

If they did this, the promise continued thus:

> *"That your days and the days of your children may be multiplied...like the days of heaven on earth."*
> (Deuteronomy 11:21)

Jesus' teaching to His disciples is, therefore, an invitation to place our trust in Him for a heaven-on-earth establishment of the kingdom of God. The amount to which God's purposes are being established on the earth is directly proportional to the degree of trust His children place in the promises He has given them. The earth was created by God as a place for man to rule under His dominion. The Bible says the creation "waits for the revealing of the sons of God" (Romans 8:19).

A foundational aspect of having the kingdom of God conferred upon believers is that our inheritance is victory over every work of the devil:

> *For this purpose the Son of God was manifested, that He might destroy the works of the devil.* (1 John 3:8)

The beauty of Jesus fulfilling His mission perfectly is that He did not come to pacify the works of the devil in our lives, but to completely *destroy them.* "Destroy" is the Greek word *lyō* defined as "to loose, to untie." Jesus made it possible to demolish every work of the devil in the lives of individuals, cities, regions, and nations. The apostle Paul would later give language to the fruit of Jesus' death and resurrection on the cross. He wrote this:

> *Having disarmed principalities and powers, He made a*
> *public spectacle of them, triumphing over them.*
> (Colossians 2:15)

Jesus set the ultimate standard for every citizen of the kingdom. He defeated every obstacle that stood in the way of fulfilling the divine mission given to Him by His Father. Jesus' victory has now become our victory. In the same way Jesus was divinely sent, so we have been divinely sent.

> *"Peace to you! As the Father has sent Me, I also send*
> *you."* (John 20:21)

Victory over every work of darkness is the inheritance of every believer! Victory is not only our inheritance, it is fundamental to how God designed us to to represent Him. When we fail to live a life of victory, we are failing to represent the kingdom in the manner God designed.

Access to a life of victory today is received in the same manner it was for Jesus when He walked on the earth, and in the same manner we entered the kingdom of God—through our faith in God.

> *For whatever is born of God overcomes the world. And*
> *this is the victory that has overcome the world—our*
> *faith.* (1 John 5:4)

Our faith in God was given to us to overcome the world and every limitation of the Babylonian system.

Our ability to walk in a life of victory or a life of limitation is based on whether or not we choose to place our faith in God. Salvation, though freely given to all, has to be received through the gift of faith. Our victory over the world system must now be accessed daily for every area of life through the currency of faith, even though it's already been won through Jesus' completed mission. Our faith in the provision Jesus made available to us enables us to overcome all the limitations of the Babylonian system. Jesus did not promise a life without conflict, but joy and a promise of victory in the midst of conflict.

> *"In the world you will have tribulation; but be of good cheer, I have overcome the world."*   (John 16:33)

In Scripture, we find explicit promises which we, as citizens of the kingdom, can not only trust but be confident for a life of victory. The God who created the universe with words, who educated Adam with His words, and who raised the dead through words, has now given us His words to trust in as the key to the life of victory He so jealously desires for us. The words of Scripture can be trusted because they have been given by the God who cannot lie and who has made Himself one with His Word.[39] God has actually declared to us that He has exalted His Word above His name![40] We cannot separate God from His Word. If we do not trust Scripture as the complete and absolute Word of God, we cannot fully trust God. We must place our

Our ability to walk in a life of victory or a life of limitation is based on whether or not we choose to place our faith in God.

faith in the following promises which are given to every citizen of the kingdom. If we do, we will live the overcoming victorious life God created us to live. The promises given in the Old Testament to the nation of Israel and Jewish people are now wonderfully and beautifully handed on to all those who are in Christ.[41] The following are promises that are the inheritance of every citizen of the kingdom of God, regardless of their assignment, culture, or time period. These promises, while certainly not exhaustive, will enable you to build a strong

---

39. See Numbers 23:19, John 1:1.
40. See Psalm 138:2.
41. See Galatians 3:13-14.

foundation for a life of victory. God mandates that we trust His Word if we are going to overcome in the same manner Jesus overcame. The following section is not an attempt to present an exhaustive teaching of these promises. I believe the promises found in Scripture stand for themselves because they are the Word of God. I have, however, included a brief exhortation of the promise and some of my personal experience in seeing that promise manifested in my life. Through a choice to be intentional and the empowerment of the Holy Spirit and the Word of God we can appropriate the following truths:

WE CAN BASE OUR ENTIRE EXISTENCE ON GOD'S WORD

God's promises about what He desires to do for us are found in the Bible. He invites humanity to trust the faithfulness of His Word. It is simple but contains eternity-changing truth. When applied, these truths will reshape our life.

Nearly twenty-four years ago while sitting in a small dorm room in my freshmen year of college, I made an intentional decision to live by the Word of God and pursue a life of deep fellowship with the Godhead. The next day, I can vividly remember sitting in a chair and telling God that I wanted to know Him like no one else had. I began talking to Him about everything that came into my mind—and I mean everything. I thought surely that at least twenty minutes had passed, but to my surprise only about five minutes had passed. It was five of the most boring minutes of my life. I remember looking up at the ceiling and thinking to myself, *How does anyone have fellowship with You? This is so boring!* However, I knew God's Word promised that He would draw near to those who drew near to Him (James 4:8), so, I kept at it. As I persistently drew near to God, God drew near to me just as He promised He would.

God's Word is a guarantee of what He has promised. His promises are an anchor of hope that we are not to be defined by our current contrary experience anymore, but rather by what He has declared to be true and possible for our lives.

The grass withers, the flower fades, but the word of our
God stands forever. (Isaiah 40:8)

For the word of the Lord is right, and all His work is
done in truth. (Psalm 33:4)

Every word of God is pure; He is a shield to those who
put their trust in Him. (Proverbs 30:5)

"Heaven and earth will pass away, but My words will by
no means pass away." (Matthew 24:35)

WE ARE A NEW CREATION AND OUR SINS ARE COMPLETELY FORGIVEN AND FORGOTTEN

Jesus' death, burial, and resurrection were so complete that as a new creation, we are not only *forgiven* of our sins, but those sins are *completely forgotten* too. If we have truly repented and believed, the God-head has no record of our sin. Jesus' death covered every sin that mankind *had ever* and *would ever* commit: immorality, idolatry, addiction, racism, hatred; all has been covered by the blood of Jesus. As a new creation, we have become part of a new race of people that never existed before. This truth is vitally important because God relates to us according to the new creature He made within us, not according to our previous life of failure and defeat.

While He is well aware of our weaknesses, He made us a new creature so He could relate to us according to where He is taking us, instead of our past and present state. Often when God speaks to me, I focus on my own weaknesses and mistakes, and then reason that I cannot move forward in what He is asking me to accomplish. Over time, however, I have come to realize that He is relating to me from my new creation, not my previous mistakes or destructive sin patterns. Knowing this helps me recognize that He is in this with me, and gives me the confidence to take the next step in faith, trusting Him.

He has not dealt with us according to our sins, nor pun-
ished us according to our iniquities. For as the heavens

25

are high above the earth, so great is His mercy toward those who fear Him; as far as the east is from the west, so far has He removed our transgressions from us.
(Psalm 103:10-12)

Who is a God like You, pardoning iniquity and passing over the transgression of the remnant of His heritage? He does not retain His anger forever, because He delights in mercy. He will again have compassion on us, and will subdue our iniquities. You will cast all our sins into the depths of the sea. (Micah 7:18-19)

Therefore, if anyone is in Christ, he is a new creation; old things have passed away; behold, all things have become new. (2 Corinthians 5:17)

WE ARE UNITED WITH CHRIST

I have always had a deep desire to experience all that was possible in the life of a believer. In that pursuit, I have yearned for a pure heart and its consequence—holy living. I have learned that the more I focused upon experiencing the Father's love and loving God with all my heart, soul, and strength, the more the choices I made lined up with God's Word and His standards of purity and righteousness.

One day, God spoke to me and said, "Live as though your life is being recorded *because it is.*" This truth helped shape and transform my daily life. Our lives are being recorded. God is divinely committed and connected to all those who are His own. In that place of ownership, He never leaves us—even in those moments when we choose to *not* trust Him or when we rebel against His Word. When we choose paths that lead to death, God is still joined to us. He is lovingly yearning to empower us to choose Him and the life He has committed to giving us from the inside-out.

Now if we died with Christ, we believe that we shall also live with Him. (Romans 6:8)

*But you are not in the flesh but in the Spirit, if indeed
the Spirit of God dwells in you. Now if anyone does not
have the Spirit of Christ, he is not His.* (Romans 8:9)

But he who is joined to the Lord is one spirit with Him.
(1 Corinthians 6:17)

*One God and Father of all, who is above all,
and through all, and in you all.* (Ephesians 4:6)

WE ARE COMPLETELY RIGHTEOUS BEFORE GOD

When Jesus looks at us, He sees Himself. No sin stands between us.
His blood has been interposed, allowing us access to the Father again.

This truth has often been challenging for me to receive and believe
in my journey in learning to trust God. I had many life experiences
which reinforced an unhealthy performance-oriented, religious mindset. When my thoughts and behavior did not measure up to the standard of God's Word, I often felt guilty and then embarrassed to engage in fellowship with God—even after sincerely repenting. I found
that I was actually projecting my own thoughts of disappointment and
discouragement onto God.

It is vitally important that we do not project our negative feel-
ings about ourselves onto God. As Jesus related to the Father as the
sinless Son, so we can continually stand before God as *sinless sons
and daughters*. We must make a daily decision to trust God, and see
ourselves in the same manner He does.

*Even the righteousness of God, through faith in Jesus
Christ, to all and on all who believe. For there is no difference.* (Romans 3:22)

*For what does the Scripture say? "Abraham believed
God, and it was accounted to him for righteousness."*
(Romans 4:3)

But of Him you are in Christ Jesus, who became for us
wisdom from God—and righteousness and sanctification
and redemption. (1 Corinthians 1:30)

For He made Him who knew no sin to be sin for us, that
we might become the righteousness of God in Him.
(2 Corinthians 5:21)

WE ARE LOVED IN THE SAME WAY JESUS WAS LOVED

Through Jesus, our relationship with the Father and the Spirit was
restored. We have been reconciled. Therefore, the Father loves us and
regards us just as He does Jesus. Jesus was called the beloved Son;
we, too, are the *beloved of God*. He is a Father who chooses to lavish
His unconditional love upon weak people; even though we are weak,
we have been fashioned to receive and live from His love. This is perhaps one of the most liberating truths I have ever experienced.

Knowing God intimately and receiving His love is the cornerstone
of my relationship with God. Often, my interaction with God is simply spent having intentional and concentrated time receiving His love.
Many times, I will wake from a nap and hear His voice whisper, "I
love you! I am very proud of you!"

And suddenly a voice came from heaven, saying, "This
is My beloved Son, in whom I am well pleased."
(Matthew 3:17)

"I in them, and You in Me; that they may be made per-
fect in one, and that the world may know that You have
sent Me, and have loved them as You have loved Me."
(John 17:23)

"And I have declared to them Your name, and will de-
clare it, that the love with which You loved Me may be in
them, and I in them." (John 17:26)

Behold what manner of love the Father has bestowed on
us, that we should be called children of God! Therefore

the world does not know us, because it did not know Him. (1 John 3:1)

WE HAVE FAVOR WITH GOD

As ambassadors, we have favor with God. Favor is defined as "kind regard, support, defense, vindication, and to promote."[42] Favor is a defining characteristic in our lives as ambassadors of Christ. It enables us to overcome the Babylonian system.

I have continually experienced the favor of God in every area of my life. God has done what was not humanly possible through His favor operating in my life. His favor has opened doors of uncommon opportunity, supernaturally brought financial resources, and allowed me to meet and have relationship with people in obvious places of authority and influence on one hand, and those I would have missed if I walked in the natural on the other. These last include mentors and others in my life with whom God connected me for His purposes.

As I have walked in this favor, I have learned some keys to seeing its operation on a daily basis:

- You must make a choice to receive the favor of God daily.

- Acknowledge His favor when you see it in operation by giving thanks.

- Live with a positive and constant expectation that His favor will be in operation everywhere in your life.

A number of years ago, God commanded me to view every situation in my life through the lens of His favor. I believe this is applicable in the life of *every believer*. In the middle of every difficult and challenging circumstance, we are challenged to trust God that the power of His favor will cause us to overcome it. God's preferential grace is upon you now to overcome every limitation and difficulty you are facing! God is more then able. Through His favor, He will!

---

42. Noah Webster, "Favor" *1828 American Dictionary of the English Language,* original facsimile edition (Chesapeake, VA: Foundation for American Christian Education, 1968).

You have granted me life and favor, and Your care has preserved my spirit. (Job 10:12)

For You, O Lord, will bless the righteous; with favor You will surround him as with a shield. (Psalm 5:12)

For his anger lasts only a moment, but his favor lasts a lifetime; Weeping may stay for the night, but rejoicing comes in the morning. (Psalm 30:5 NIV)

For the Lord God is a sun and shield; the Lord will give grace and glory; no good thing will He withhold from those who walk uprightly. (Psalm 84:11)

GOD EMPOWERS US FOR EVERY GOOD WORK

God has chosen to live *inside* each and every ambassador in His kingdom. He is more than justified in asking us to do what is impossible because of that fact, enabling us to fulfill what He has asked. It is His power dwelling in us that moves on our behalf when we choose to follow the predetermined path He has ordained before the foundation of the earth. Our life in Him will include inconvenience, challenges, and plenty of invitations from Him to do what we believe is not possible.

I have had countless experiences in which I believed myself to be unqualified, unable, or bereft of the time and resources I needed to do what I knew God was asking. Yet every time I obeyed, I discovered a power working in me that was not of this world and certainly not rooted in my own strength. As His ambassadors acting on His behalf, we are authorized and empowered for every good work.

Trust in the Lord, and do good; dwell in the land, and feed on His faithfulness. (Psalm 37:3)

For we are His workmanship, created in Christ Jesus for good works, which God prepared beforehand that we should walk in them. (Ephesians 2:10)

I can do all things through Christ who strengthens me.
(Philippians 4:13)

This is a faithful saying, and these things I want you to affirm constantly, that those who have believed in God should be careful to maintain good works. These things are good and profitable to men. (Titus 3:8)

Make you complete in every good work to do His will, working in you what is well pleasing in His sight, through Jesus Christ, to whom be glory forever and ever. Amen. (Hebrews 13:21)

WE CAN TRUST GOD TO HAVE COMPLETE VICTORY OVER SIN

The will of God is that you never struggle with sin. Victory over sin is our inheritance. Jesus died to free us from that cycle. While many believers will agree that God has made it possible to live in victory over all sin, a large percentage of believers continue to struggle with continual sinful habits and addictions. At times, these addictions and sinful habits can be the result of our own choices before and after becoming born-again; others can be the result of generational issues that have been passed down to us through our bloodline.

When I was born-again, many chains of sin and addiction were broken immediately. However, I still continued to struggle with certain mindsets and habits that I would choose easily, even though I knew they violated the standards of God's Word. Deliverance ministry, which we will look at next, was pivotal and necessary in me so that I could experience complete freedom. The abundant life Jesus promised is one of complete victory over sin and it is the life that I am now experiencing on a daily basis. The following are some keys to living a life of complete victory over sin:

- Deliverance and ongoing prayer ministry.

- Feeding your heart and mind on the Word of God (in other words, renewing your mind).

- Walking in covenant relationship with a family community.

For sin shall not have dominion over you, for you are
not under law but under grace.   (Romans 6:14)

But thanks be to God, who gives us the victory through
our Lord Jesus Christ.   (1 Corinthians 15:57)

DELIVERANCE SHOULD BE PART OF THE SALVATION EXPERIENCE FOR EVERY BELIEVER

Deliverance ministry is one of the most neglected *and misunderstood* components of kingdom ministry. While deliverance ministry is just one gift God has given to us to walk in freedom, I believe it is a ministry that is necessary for every believer if we are to walk in complete victory over sin.

In my own desire to live and experience complete victory over sin, I sought after and received deliverance and prayer ministry. Each year, I purposefully receive prayer ministry as part of my ongoing desire to live a life of continual freedom. I can testify that God has given me the grace to live in complete victory over addiction, struggle, and torment. The benefits of deliverance are manifold. Deliverance ministry provides the following benefits:

Life lived outside of the context of knowing God is foundationally defeated.

- Brings true repentance of sin.

- Identifies its root causes, bringing us into an experience of increased freedom.

- Tracks tendencies toward possible iniquity.

- Opens our eyes and heals our heart as we allow the Holy Spirit to expose our soul and transform us on a deeper level.

- Helps us trust God more as we allow Him to touch and heal us.

- Humbles us as we submit to Jesus.

> *These things I have spoken to you, that in Me you may have peace. In the world you will have tribulation; but be of good cheer, I have overcome the world.*
> (John 16:33)

> *Then Jesus said to those Jews who believed Him, "If you abide in My word, you are My disciples indeed. And you shall know the truth, and the truth shall make you free."* (John 8:31-32)

WE CAN HAVE GOD'S FAITH, AND ALL THINGS ARE POSSIBLE WITH GOD'S FAITH

God's faith has been given to us as a gift, so that what we believe about God can become a reality in our lives. Over twenty years ago, I read John 14:12 and began pursuing, not only doing the works Jesus did, but doing *greater works*. God has been faithful to allow me to experience His miraculous power firsthand around the world.

On one occasion, I was in Brazil with a team from around the world doing an outreach in a small town. As the day came to an end, we were invited into the small home of a family with a young man about twenty years of age who (from what I was told) had never walked in his whole life. Our team shared a simple gospel message with the family. We asked them if they wanted to repent of their sins and receive Jesus Christ as their Lord and Savior. The father declined our invitation. He went on to say that if he could, he would take his son's place, so that his son could walk and he would be paralyzed instead.

I told him that the good news was that he did not have to take his son's place, but that we would pray and believe God to do a miracle. I began to pray with a small group from our team. After praying, the young man did not show any physical signs of change. I asked God

33

what to do. He gave me a very specific word, telling me to wash the young man's feet. Then I heard God say, "If you will lay down your life for people, I will continually do what I am about to do for this young man."

After we washed the young man's feet, we prayed again and the young man slowly began to walk for the first time in his life. Shortly after this, the entire family surrendered their lives to God. God is a God of His Word. God will do the impossible if you choose to trust Him!

> *"For with God nothing will be impossible."* (Luke 1:37)

> *And Jesus, answering, said to them, "Have God's faith."*
> (Mark 11:22 BBE)

> *Jesus said to him, "If you can believe, all things are possible to him who believes."* (Mark 9:23)

> *But without faith it is impossible to please Him, for he who comes to God must believe that He is, and that He is a rewarder of those who diligently seek Him.*
> (Hebrews 11:6)

WE CAN KNOW THAT OUR FAITH IN GOD OVERCOMES THE WORLD

Even though we live in a world that experiences the consequences of man's disobedience and the resulting Babylonian system, we do not have to be subject to its evil. If we want to live according to God's divine design, we must live with a sense of responsibility and obligation toward all people. As a citizen of His kingdom, God has empowered me to live in complete freedom over this world system. I am required to pursue an abundant life and be an example of what that looks like too. I am *in* this world but not *of* it. My entire life is devoted to offering invitations to those who have yet to choose to surrender to Jesus.

> *For the Lord your God is He who goes with you, to fight for you against your enemies, to save you.*
> (Deuteronomy 20:4)

"These things I have spoken to you, that in Me you may have peace. In the world you will have tribulation; but be of good cheer, I have overcome the world."

(John 16:33)

For whatever is born of God overcomes the world. And this is the victory that has overcome the world—our faith. (1 John 5:4)

Yet in all these things we are more than conquerors through Him who loved us. (Romans 8:37)

Having disarmed principalities and powers, He made a public spectacle of them, triumphing over them in it.

(Colossians 2:15)

WE CAN HAVE AN ETERNAL FRIENDSHIP WITH THE LORD

Our life cannot produce fruit beyond the foundation established within us through our friendship with God. His greatest desire right now is to find people who will relentlessly choose to live as His friends. The victorious life God has called us to live cannot be lived without this deep, ongoing fellowship.

My life has been defined by relentlessly pursuing friendship with God. Having found my greatest satisfaction and pleasure in knowing Him, life does not make any sense outside of fellowship with Him. Living without that would be like leaving my home without wearing clothes. It would be lunacy and self-destructive. Life lived outside of the context of knowing God is foundationally defeated.

One thing I have desired of the Lord that will I seek: that I may dwell in the house of the Lord all the days of my life, to behold the beauty of the Lord, and to inquire in His temple. (Psalm 27:4)

"And this is eternal life, that they may know You, the only true God, and Jesus Christ whom You have sent."
(John 17:3)

And the Scripture was fulfilled which says, "Abraham believed God, and it was accounted to him for righteousness." And he was called the friend of God.
(James 2:23)

...that I may know Him and the power of His resurrection, and the fellowship of His sufferings, being conformed to His death. (Philippians 3:10)

WE CAN TRUST GOD TO FIND OUR ASSIGNMENT FOR OUR TIME ON EARTH

Purpose is common to all. Every human being has a God-ordained reason for living. When we choose to continually surrender to God and find our greatest pleasure in knowing Him, we will also discover our purpose and His assignment for us on earth.

I have yet to meet anyone who is sincerely seeking God with all of their heart and desiring to live by His Word that does not have at least some understanding of their purpose. Even after we begin to understand our purpose and walk it out, God will still continually require great trust in Him. The more deeply I move into my purpose, the greater degree of trust God requires. It is crucial that we discover our purpose because God shapes the world according to the specific assignments in which His people walk.

You will show me the path of life; in your presence is fullness of joy; at your right hand are pleasures forevermore. (Psalm 16:11)

"Before I formed you in the womb I knew you; before you were born I sanctified you; I ordained you a prophet to the nations." (Jeremiah 1:5)

For I know the thoughts that I think toward you, says the Lord, thoughts of peace and not of evil, to give you a future and a hope. (Jeremiah 29:11)

For whom He foreknew, He also predestined to be conformed to the image of His Son, that He might be the firstborn among many brethren. Moreover whom He predestined, these He also called; whom He called, these He also justified; and whom He justified, these He also glorified. (Romans 8:29-30)

WE CAN TRUST GOD TO GUIDE US AND SHARE HIS THOUGHTS WITH US

The God who knows all things is committed to freely sharing His wisdom and thoughts. One of the roles of the Holy Spirit is to search the mind of Christ to share His thoughts, purposes, and intentions. When we have made the choice to commit our works to God, our commitment to trust God opens His thoughts and intentions to us every day.

One of the most common ways I receive God's thoughts happens when I am engaging in worship. I often suddenly think of a person or situation. I used to think these impressions were distractions, keeping me from my focus upon God. But over time, I realized that *God was giving me His thoughts*. Often, they are clear words to me, but at other times, they are as simple as having someone I had not thought about in many years pop into my mind. These quick impressions lead to further dialogue with God and His subsequent direction. God delights in sharing His thoughts and intentions with His children.

How precious also are your thoughts to me, O God! How great is the sum of them! If I should count them, they would be more in number than the sand. (Psalm 139:17-18a)

"However, when He, the Spirit of truth, has come, He will guide you into all truth; for He will not speak on His own authority, but whatever He hears He will speak; and He will tell you things to come." (John 16:13)

> *For "who has known the mind of the Lord that he may instruct Him?" But we have the mind of Christ.*
>
> (1 Corinthians 2:16)

> *Set your mind on things above, not on things on the earth.* (Colossians 3:2)

WE CAN KNOW (AND LIVE BY) THE VOICE OF GOD

The voice of God is a gift to every citizen of the kingdom, providing wisdom, guidance, and understanding. God's voice is also a key, so that we can declare what He is saying. As we declare His words, His word becomes our future.

A key aspect of knowing God's voice is the ability that His voice gives us in ministering to the world around us. In 2008, I was ministering for the first time in the Philippines. One morning, I was asked to speak at a Full Gospel Businessmen's Fellowship meeting at the home of a local doctor. After a brief time of worship, the meeting was turned over to me. The Holy Spirit clearly instucted me to minister a word to this doctor. As I began to minister the word of the Lord to him, the glory of God filled the small room in which we had gathered. The doctor began to weep. He then told the group that he now knew what he needed to do.

Within that year, the doctor ran for mayor of his town and defeated an incumbent corrupt politician who had been in office for over twenty years. The doctor testified that the word he received from God had been crucial in his decision to run for mayor and his very unlikely victory.

As kingdom ambassadors, it is our responsibility to know the voice of God and be proficient in ministering His Word to the world around us. This should be part of our lifestyle. Knowing His voice is critical to changing the earth so it becomes as God intends.

> *And Pharoah said to Joseph, "I have had a dream, and there is no one who can interpret it. But I have heard it said of you that you can understand a dream, to interpret it."* (Genesis 41:15)

*But He answered and said, "It is written, 'Man shall
not live by bread alone, but by every word that proceeds
from the mouth of God.'"* (Matthew 4:4)

*"My sheep hear My voice, and I know them, and they fol-
low Me."* (John 10:27)

*So then faith comes by hearing, and hearing by the word
of God.* (Romans 10:17)

WE CAN TRUST GOD TO PROVIDE EVERYTHING WE WILL EVER NEED

God created humanity to receive from Him all that we would ever
need for eternity. God's Word has promised resources and provision
for all who would choose to live under His dominion. The Babylonian
system has a very defined economic system designed to keep people
under constant pressure and with very few experiencing abundance.
One of the fruits of the Babylonian system is coveting among the
masses. The good news is that the kingdom of God has a very defined
economic system too. It is designed to resource its ambassadors with
everything they would ever need.

Over seventeen years ago, God mandated me to begin the ministry
I am currently leading. At the time, I had perhaps five hundred dollars
to my name and no means of regular support. I began to live with the
conviction that God would be my Source. I searched the Scriptures
and spoke with God on how His economic system functioned. I also
began to intently listen to leaders who were experiencing abundant
provision in their lives and ministries. The following are key to partic-
ipating in God's economic system. I have applied these principles and
have seen God's hand of mighty provision, not only in my personal
life but also in the ministry that He has entrusted to me.

- God will resource you through a variety of different methods,
  but He is *the* Source for your total supply.

- With God as your Source, you do not need to manipulate,
  pressure, or try to make a way for your own provision.

- God has instituted the giving of finances as an act of worship that allows you to recognize Him as your total Source.

- Stewardship and the fruit of the Spirit of self-control are essential disciplines in God's economic system.

- Tithing is giving *the first* 10% of all the money God has placed in our hands to the community in which God has called us as members.

- Giving other offerings over and above our tithe in response to the voice of God is the norm.

- God has made specific promises to those who trust Him with His tithe and our offerings.

- Tithing and the giving of offerings are not to be one-time events, but a lifestyle for citizens of the kingdom.

- We can give our offering as seed and expect a financial harvest.

- "God always remembers a seed sown." —Dr. Jerry Savelle

"While the earth remains, seedtime and harvest, cold and heat, winter and summer, and day and night shall not cease." (Genesis 8:22)

The Lord is my shepherd; I shall not want. (Psalm 23:1)

"Bring all the tithe into the storehouse, that there may be food in My house, and try Me now in this," says the Lord of hosts, "if I will not open for you the windows of heaven and pour out for you such blessing that there will not be room enough to receive it." (Malachi 3:10)

As His divine power has given to us all things that pertain to life and godliness, through the knowledge of Him who called us by glory and virtue. (2 Peter 1:3)

IT IS THE WILL OF GOD TO PROSPER US AND BRING US WEALTH

The primary goal of God's economic system is not simply the accumulation of wealth. God's goal for every ambassador of His kingdom is that we would be conformed to the image of Jesus. As we walk out the process of becoming like Him, a fruit of that is abundance and prosperity.

Wealth can be defined differently according to our culture and nation. For example, the average American can own one car and not be considered wealthy, while the average person owning a vehicle in Singapore would be considered wealthy because of the extraordinary cost behind it. I will always remember when God spoke to me many years ago and said, "Abner, if I have your heart, I will give you the world." God never lacks and is able to consistently supply the needs of humanity. God desires that as we accumulate wealth, we would demonstrate His nature to the world by being extravagant givers. Our ability to give like God is facilitated when we think like God. Before I began to see great breakthroughs in this area, God first began to teach me how to think like Him. Our giving as kingdom citizens should never be tied to what is actually in our bank accounts. Our giving follows God's commands. Giving like God as a lifestyle is, therefore, the practice of learning to trust God. As we learn to give like God, we are promised that, like God, we will never lack.

Many years ago, I was ministering at two different meetings. I knew I had many bills due and I did not know how they would (or could) be paid. After the first service was completed, it was reported to me how much they had given me as a love offering, I remember being terribly disappointed because it was far below what I was believing God for. In the second service, an offering was received *before* I ministered. I had a strong impression that I was to *give* the entire offering that I had just received. Initially this impression came as a tremendous challenge, but I sensed a tremendous freedom and joy to be able to give the offering as an act of worship, so I did. That week, God supernaturally supplied more than I needed to pay all my bills. God has been continually faithful to me because He is faithful to His Word. Perhaps you have never understood that God has a particular economic system for His people or you are living under constant financial pressure and strain. *Start where you are.* Each of us begins in a different place financially. Perhaps you have always lived from paycheck to paycheck. God's Word is available to deliver you! Perhaps you are constantly accumulating more and more debt. God's Word is available to deliver you! Perhaps you have never gone on a vacation. God's Word is available to bring you the provision you need. Maybe you have no idea how God could give you the resources to pay for your children's college tuition. God's Word has the answer to your resource problems.

As we walk in the experience of greater financial freedom, we begin to live above the limitations of this world system. Our desire to become wealthy should not only be anchored in God's promise to us, but in our motivation to become a resource to the world around us. God is looking for people who will partner with Him to become storehouses in their sphere of influence.

> *"And you shall remember the Lord your God, for it is He who gives you power to get wealth, that He may establish His covenant which He swore to your fathers, as it is this day."* (Deuteronomy 8:18)

> *The blessing of the Lord makes one rich, and He adds no sorrow with it.* (Proverbs 10:22)

> *The wise have wealth and luxury, but fools spend whatever they get.* (Proverbs 21:20 NLT)

> *Don't love money; be satisfied with what you have. For God has said, "I will never fail you. I will never abandon you."* (Hebrews 13:5 NLT)

WE CAN TRUST GOD TO LIVE WITHOUT SICKNESS AND DISEASE

Although we will participate in the sufferings of Jesus in our lives, sickness and disease are not *from God*. God has never (and will never) place sickness or disease upon someone to teach or train them in some aspect of the kingdom. While He works all things according to His will, sickness and disease are not part of God's plan for the believer. God will deliver His people as an answer to the prayer of faith, standing on His Word and through medicine. Medical science and God's Word and His kingdom are not opposed to each other.

As a young man, I suffered from terrible allergies. I had a continual cold, even in the middle of the summer. One day after returning from a ministry trip, I was feeling really run down. I cried out to God to deliver me as it was becoming increasingly difficult to travel and minister. At some point in the middle of my struggles with allergies, I had promised my mother to see a doctor. When I did, the doctor walked into the room and exclaimed, "You look terrible!" (I was actually feeling a lot better than I had in many days.) In that appointment the doctor gave me a simple vitamin C shot. On that day I began to trust God for complete deliverance from all allergies. From that day forward, I began to feel better and better, and a few months later, I was completely delivered of all of it. I no longer suffer the terrible effects of constant allergies. For most of my life, I have walked in divine health, and so has most of my immediate family. I believe walking in divine health is not simply believing God at His Word, but also trusting Him to give you the power to eat a healthy diet and exercise on a regular basis.

> *And said, "If you diligently heed the voice of*
> *the Lord your God and do what is right in His sight,*
> *give ear to His commandments and keep all His stat-*
> *utes, I will put none of the diseases on you which I have*
> *brought on the Egyptians. For I am the Lord who heals*
> *you."* (Exodus 15:26)

> *But He was wounded for our transgressions, He*
> *was bruised for our iniquities; the chastisement for our*
> *peace was upon Him, and by His stripes we are healed.*
> (Isaiah 53:5)

> *How God anointed Jesus of Nazareth with the Holy*
> *Spirit and with power, who went about doing good and*

*healing all who were oppressed by the devil, for God
was with Him.* (Acts 10:38)

*Beloved, I pray that you may prosper in all things and
be in health, just as your soul prospers.* (3 John 1:2)

WE CAN TRUST GOD TO HAVE A SOUND MIND AND LIVE FREE OF TORMENT AND DEPRESSION

As kingdom citizens, we will not be exempt from difficulty or storms. However, many believers live defeated lives because they have not learned to renew their minds or cast down the thoughts and lies of the enemy. The lies that believers trust often result in them experiencing torment on a regular basis and also result in sickness and disease. It is the disposition of our hearts in the middle of difficulty and chaos that allows us to live above circumstances, difficulties, and trouble. If we do not train our hearts to stay focused on God and His Word, we will be ineffective in walking in the authority God has given us, which He wants us to use to define the world around us.

The choice to renew our minds and maintain proper focus must be made daily. One day, I was headed on a trip to minister at youth camp at the beach. As I was driving on the interstate, panicky thoughts about what could go wrong in my life and ministry began to take hold of me. In the middle of the onslaught, I simply declared aloud, "God, I trust You!" As I said those words, an overwhelming sense of peace and grace flooded my mind and heart. A few moments later, those same thoughts attacked my mind a second time. I declared again, "God, I trust You!" and it ceased. A sound mind is essential to living the overcoming life!

*You will keep him in perfect peace, whose mind is
stayed on You, because he trusts in You.* (Isaiah 26:3)

*Casting down arguments and every high thing that
exalts itself against the knowledge of God, bringing
every thought into captivity to the obedience of Christ.*
(2 Corinthians 10:5)

Let the peace of Christ rule in your hearts, since as members of one body you were called to peace. And be thankful. (Colossians 3:15 NIV)

For God has not given us a spirit of fear, but of power and of love and of a sound mind. (2 Timothy 1:7)

WE CAN TRUST GOD THAT WE WILL DO GREATER WORKS THAN JESUS DID

A key to walking and replicating the works of Jesus is to educate yourself according to the Word of God, so you know what is from God and what is from the devil. When we are convinced that sickness, disease, poverty, depression, and the like are from the enemy, then that knowledge births a desire within us to see the reality of what God has promised in His Word. We hold fast to God's truth in the face of every lie. To be truly compassionate toward others, we must shoulder the responsibility that we have been authorized by God Himself to bring freedom and wholeness to people. The miracles demonstrated in our lives are a sign of God's compassion and love for everyone. The youngest to the oldest in the kingdom of God can do the works of God.

After ministering, I am often told that people feel like a million pounds have been lifted off their shoulders. Life inside the kingdom of God is not always easy, but life outside the kingdom is a down payment for hell. May we seek to do the works of Jesus, so that others may experience the abundant life He died to give them.

And when He had called His twelve disciples to Him, He gave them power over unclean spirits, to cast them out, and to heal all kinds of sickness and all kinds of disease. (Matthew 10:1)

"Most assuredly, I say to you, he who believes in Me, the works that I do he will do also; and greater works than these he will do, because I go to My Father." (John 14:12)

"And these signs will follow those who believe: In My name they will cast out demons; they will speak with new tongues; they will take up serpents; and if they drink anything deadly, it will by no means hurt them; they will lay hands on the sick, and they will recover."   (Mark 16:17-18)

By stretching out Your hand to heal, and that signs and wonders may be done through the name of Your holy Servant Jesus.   (Acts 4:30)

GOD'S SPOKEN WORDS CAN MOVE MOUNTAINS

The words out of our mouth define the level of victory we experience. We must declare the world of victory that we want to live in before we experience what we have spoken. I encourage you to renew your mind in these truths: God cannot lie to you, and you can have what you say. A critical aspect of my life of fellowship with God is declaring His Word over different aspects of life. I declare that all unsaved relatives will become born-again; I declare that the blessing of the Lord defines every part of my life; I declare that I will love all people as God loves people; I declare that God is giving me increased boldness to speak and do the works of Jesus. Many times, I have declared God's truth years before I lived in the experience of that truth.

Faith is the only currency that connects humanity with God.

As this ministry began to grow, I began to see the need to hire help to adminstrate and organize the ministry. While we did not have the resources to do this, we had something more powerful: God's Word coming out of my mouth. As a prophetic act, I placed a chair next to the desk in my home office and began to declare that God was sending me an administrative assistant. On many of these occasions, I would hear the voice of the enemy saying, "You are crazy!" "You don't even have enough for yourself!" "This will never happen!" I kept at it anyway. Within about a year and a half, God graciously provided our first administrative assistant who helped bring us to a greater place of efficiency and effectiveness. Living a life of victory as an ambassador of the kingdom of God is learning to consistently declare God's Word.

> *"For assuredly, I say to you, whoever says to this mountain, 'Be removed and be cast into the sea,' and does not doubt in his heart, but believes that those things he says will be done, he will have whatever he says."*
> (Mark 11:23)

> *Jesus answered and said to them, "This is the work of God, that you believe in Him whom He sent."*
> (John 6:29)

> *"It is the Spirit who gives life; the flesh profits nothing. The words that I speak to you are spirit, and they are life."*
> (John 6:63)

> *Who through faith subdued kingdoms, worked righteousness, obtained promises, stopped the mouths of lions.*
> (Hebrews 11:33)

This chapter was written for the purpose of presenting biblical promises that are the inheritance of every citizen of the kingdom. God's passion is for humanity to live as He intended and we can do this by inheriting these promises. As we live in these promises and overcome the evils of the Babylonian system, we not only embrace the abundant life Jesus promised but we also serve as faithful witnesses of the kingdom of God.

As you read through this chapter, perhaps you saw some of the promises of Scripture in a manner you had never seen before. Or maybe you feel discouraged because even though you love God with all your heart, your experience is below what God has promised. It is also possible you have been believing God for complete healing in your body for many years and have yet to see your healing manifest. Or that even after many years of being born-again, you still find yourself terribly enslaved to one particular sin or group of sins. You may have experienced terrible financial hardships for months, perhaps even years, and do not see how things could ever change. Do not lose hope. God will empower you to stand—and keep standing—on His Word. For many of you, the simplest answer to your challenges is to simply keep trusting God and standing on His Word.

My purpose for presenting these promises is simply to declare what God has said is possible for all of His people! God's heart of love and kindness is extended toward you, regardless of your current experience or previous choices. I do not know any believer in the body of Christ that is experiencing the absolute fullness of God and all that He has made available to us. So remember that the Father is not judging or condemning you. Instead, He is *with you* in your current situation, ready to enable that which He has declared to be pos-

Intentional surrender opens the door to walking in the power of God's faith.

sible. I encourage you to take intentional time with your Father to possibly discover any places in which repentance or a shift in your focus is needed. Doing this will put you on track to inherit the promises God has made available to you. If you are married and you and your spouse are not experiencing God's promises, I encourage you to do this as a couple or even as a family.

I want to conclude this chapter by listing eight possible reasons why people do not live an overcoming life, the kind God created for them to live. Once again, this particular list is qualitative, not exhaustive.

- God is a part of your life, but not your primary pursuit (Matthew 6:33).

- You live in continual disobedience (1 Samuel 15:23).

- You do not understand true repentance (1 John 1:9-10).

- You are unaware that God's promises are for you personally (Hosea 4:6).

- You harbor unforgiveness in your heart that has possibly developed into a root of bitterness (Mark 11:25, Hebrews 12:25).

- You have embraced a worldview in which God's promises are *not for all believers today* (Matthew 16:6).

- You embrace God's promises as being for today, but are unstable and double-minded (James 1:2-7).

- You do not believe you are worthy to receive God's promises.

Recognizing our heart's condition is the Holy Spirit's job. Leading us into all the truth is also His domain. If you know that you are not experiencing the fullness of a life in the center of God's will, take some time right now to pray and ask Him to help you. He will answer, and He's got real solutions. You can trust Him to be your Helper.

Key Concepts from Chapter 3

- God's divine design that humanity would be His ambassadors on earth has never changed.

- Jesus' life, death, and resurrection did not complete the task of advancing the kingdom, but modeled what God has now made possible for all people.

- Our faith in God was given to us so we could overcome the world.

- When we overcome the world, we represent the kingdom of God in the manner God intended.

- God's desire is that mankind would bring heaven to earth as we represent His kingdom.

- Essential to that process is our choice to believe the promises of Scripture that God has made available.

- God has made Himself One with His Word and His Word can be trusted.

CHAPTER 4

Building Our
Foundation Properly

But let each one take heed how he builds on it.
(1 Corinthians 3:10)

April 6, 2020
Words from Heaven

THIS IS THE SEASON *in which I am resetting and repurposing My people. Many of My people have been mistaken and thought they built their foundation correctly. They thought they were established in faith. But I say to My people: I desire to build your faith for eternity. I desire to build you to withstand any assault and evil from the enemy, so I am repositioning My people so that you will be rooted and grounded on the sure foundation of love, Me, My Word, and My voice.*

This will be a season in which I will make sure My voice and Word are known to those with a pure heart and sincere desire to build their house according to the Rock. So I say to My people: Be sure to build your house on the Rock of My Word, My voice, and obedience, even in the most elementary things. For as you stand upon the Rock and are sure to position your foundation on the Rock, I will expand and stretch you in territory that has never been explored by My people before. It will even go beyond what the prophets have spoken concerning it. So I say to My people: Build correctly so that you may be established to receive the increase and the great expansion I am releasing to My people in the coming seasons.

Faith in God is the master key to live on the earth as God intended. The "measure of faith" is given to each one—not only as the gift for entrance into the kingdom, but also to live in the kingdom of God. Faith is the only currency that connects humanity with God. The writer of Hebrews declared:

> *But without faith it is impossible to please Him.*
>
> (Hebrews 11:6a)

One the beauties of the way God relates to us is that He gives us everything He requires for us to live the way He intended. Humanity can only give back to God what He has first given to us as a gift. Having empowered us to do what He has required of us, God holds us responsible for our own development. The apostle Paul commanded us to "work out your own salvation with fear and trembling" (Philippians 2:12). Faith, the master key in God's kingdom, is crucial to the development of our life in God. God has granted us the honor and privilege of trusting Him as our Source of all things. Learning to walk by faith is not a destination but a journey in exploring the heart of God and His gracious intentions toward us.

A foundation is defined as the basis or groundwork of an edifice.[43] A foundation is an essential aspect of any structure. If a foundation is flawed, the structure is destined for complications. Many believers attempt to deal with the symptoms of a flawed foundation instead of the actual root issue. Many years ago as God began to teach me about the value of building my spiritual foundation properly, I asked a contracter to explain the importance of the foundation in the building of homes. The man told me that he no longer even attempts to fix flawed foundations beause of the many problems associated with that task. Now he simply begins again, by digging a new foundation, rather

---

43. Noah Webster, "Foundation" *1828 American Dictionary of the English Language,* original facsimile edition (Chesapeake, VA: Foundation for American Christian Education, 1968).

than trying to fix a flawed one. The process of building fresh from the beginning was much easier.

Our development in God is often likened to that of a house.[44] In the Sermon on the Mount, Jesus taught that only two classes of people exist in the earth—those building on the rock and those building on the sand. While everyone would face storms, it was only the person building a house on the rock whose house would stand in the storm.[45] Whether or not you are building correctly or a storm has already destroyed your spiritual house, the desire of God is to enable you to build your life properly. In the following chapter, we will explore foundational principles that are essential to not only begin to walk by faith, but actually live a lifestyle of faith. As we develop and practice these principles as a lifestyle, we will build our lives according to God's divine design. Each one is necessary to a healthy ambassador of the kingdom and each one is powerful in the fruit it brings.

SURRENDER

Our life is the result of a great variety of factors and influences, including, but not limited to: culture, economic status, family environment, education, and choices. God's grace is already working to orchestrate our lives according to His divine design, even before we are conceived. However, God's purpose for our lives cannot take full effect until we make the choice to intentionally surrender our lives to Him. That choice of intentional surrender opens the door to walking in the power of God's faith. God's desire is to take responsibility for every aspect of our lives. His ownership of our lives cannot commence until we surrender to His leadership. Our choice of intentional surrender is pivotal to building a life of faith on the appropriate foundation. Intentional surrender is the cornerstone to a life of faith.

Our surrender to God is not based on blind trust. Our surrender is based on God's integrity; it is based on who God has declared Himself to be and the love and kindness He extends to us. The enemy—through lies, propaganda, and inaccurate representation by the body

---

44.   See Luke 14:28, 1 Corinthians 3:9-13.
45.   See Matthew 7:24-27.

of Christ—has sought to keep mankind from discovering the true nature and beauty of God. God's primary intention for humanity is that the goodness He extends to us would lead us to repentance.[46] Jesus declared it in this famous verse:

> *"For God so loved the world that He gave His only begotten Son, that whoever believes in Him should not perish but have everlasting life."*   (John 3:16)

God's loving-kindness is always extended to humanity with the intention and desire that people would simply surrender to Him.

When Jesus called three of His disciples to surrender to Him, He did so only after demonstrating His goodness to them. He gave them distinct instructions on how to catch fish after they had spent all night catching nothing. After seeing the abundance of fish that came, Peter responded, "Depart from me, for I am a sinful man, O Lord" (Luke 5:8). In the presence of Jesus, Peter feared being unworthy, yet the next words of Jesus were simply, *"Do not be afraid.* From now on, you will catch men" (Luke 5:10, emphasis mine).

God's desire is that our teaching and training take place within the context of community.

Perhaps many of us, like Peter, feel unworthy and fearful when we hear the call to surrender. Without an intentional choice to surrender to God, we are bound to the devil, his demons, and the Babylonian system they have built on the earth. We serve anything to which we are enslaved. What we serve is what motivates our behavior. Peter mistakenly thought that his current lifestyle disqualified him from a life in God. Yet, the command from Jesus was simply not to be afraid and surrender to his God-given purpose for living. Intentional surrender to God breaks humanity free from our previous failures and sin.

---

46.   See Romans 2:4.

The call to surrender did not promise a life of ease and comfort. We know that Peter's life ended as a martyr for the cause for which he intentionally surrendered.

Fear is one of the defining characteristics of the Babylonian system. Fear seeks to keep people out of the kingdom of God. Despite becoming a new creation, fear will try to render you ineffective in the purposes of God. Fear manifests itself in a variety of ways: fear of failure, fear of poverty, fear of the future, fear of rejection, fear of loss, fear of being disappointed, fear of pain, fear of the unknown, and the list goes on. The command from Jesus was one of purpose and intention. He knew that the greatest obstacle to intentional surrender and trust in God is fear.

Often, humanity's greatest fear is to admit that they are inadequate in realizing the reason for their existence alone. True life and freedom can only be found in surrendering to God. That choice allows

> **That all His followers would reproduce Jesus' ministry through their individual assignments is God's cornerstone goal.**

us to live life from a place of complete surrender. Yet, the lie that often keeps people from full surrender is the fear that they will lose their life as they know it! But that is the very point of the invitation by God to full intentional surrender. One cannot find the life God offers without a surrender of the life you are currently living. Jesus declared:

> *"If anyone desires to come after Me, let him deny himself, and take up his cross, and follow Me. For whoever desires to save his life will lose it, **but whoever loses his life for My sake will find it.**"*
> (Matthew 16:24-25, emphasis mine)

Surrender opens the door to the kingdom of God and allows us to live the life of freedom offered in it. The call to surrender is not a one-time event, but a choice that sets into motion a new lifestyle that Jesus modeled, taught, and demonstrated. Luke records that "they forsook all and *followed Him"* (Luke 5:11, emphasis mine). The choice to surrender gives us a new nature and the ability to learn a new way of living in the kingdom of God. Surrender is the only posture that allows us to correctly follow God. God has made Himself one with His Word and His Word can be trusted.

The choice to intentionally surrender does not mean we have "arrived" or are fully mature, but it is the right foundation to correctly relating to God. It positions us in the journey so we can become mature and bear much fruit.

TRAINING AND EQUIPPING

Jesus welcomed a diverse group of disciples into a community in which they were completely accepted, despite their character flaws, radical political affiliations, or the fact that one was a hated tax collector. Jesus took complete responsibility for developing them in this new way of living known as the kingdom of God. They were continually challenged to believe correctly. As they followed Jesus, they lacked nothing. In fact, Jesus promised them:

> *"Assuredly, I say to you, there is no one who has left house or parents or brothers or wife or children, for the sake of the kingdom of God, who shall not receive many times more in this present time, and in the age to come eternal life."* (Luke 18:29-30)

This new way of living in the kingdom of God, in which faith is critical, must be learned, developed, and cultivated. No disciple, regardless of calling or assignment, can bypass a lifestyle of training and continual development. Jesus trained His disciples under the old covenant, which He came to fulfill. While we live and operate under the new covenant, the way in which Jesus trained His disciples gives us understanding into the manner in which God desires to train and equip us in the life of faith.

When we become born-again, each of us receives the measure of faith.[47] One of God's desires for every believer is that the measure of

---

47. See Romans 12:3; Ephesians 2:8-10.

faith He has given us would grow. Growing in faith is necessary if we are going to live the life God pre-ordained for us before we were born. A kingdom citizen who never develops (or remains weak in faith) will live far below what God has made available. An inability to develop strong faith will also cause us to live defeated and at the mercy of circumstances and difficulties.

A LIFE OF FELLOWSHIP

A life of faith begins with the call to build one's life on the Great Commandment. When asked which was the greatest commandment, Jesus answered:

> *"You shall love the Lord your God with all your heart, with all your soul, and with all your mind. This is the first and great commandment."*
> (Matthew 22:37-38)

The call to know God is what Jesus called the first and greatest commandment. It is the first and greatest commandment because it will define our existence for eternity. The invitation to love God with our whole heart was not a casual one. It was an invitation to walk with Him, to talk with Him, and to hear the deep things that the Father wanted to reveal through Him to them.

The heart of God longs to have friends in the earth who prioritize their life to know Him and live a lifestyle of deep fellowship with Him. It is in the context of fellowship with God that we learn by experience of the beauty and kindness of God. When we know God by experience, it releases boldness within us to trust and act fearlessly in response to Him. God intended that as we know Him, we would trust Him.

It is only when we know God properly that we can love our neighbor properly. After declaring the first and greatest commandment, Jesus declared,

> *"And the second is like it: 'You shall love your neighbor as yourself.'"*
> (Matthew 22:39)

As kingdom citizens, we are required to love our neighbor exactly as we love ourselves. Loving others exactly as we love ourselves is essential to living a life of faith. The life of faith God requires of us cannot function without true love operating in our lives. In His epistle to the church at Corinth, Paul wrote that despite having faith to move mountains, if we did not have love, we had nothing.[48]

HEARING

One of the primary methods Jesus used to communicate the message of the kingdom was through teaching the Word of God. Jesus taught the multitudes from the mountaintop, in the synagogue, and in people's homes.[49] The disciples He originally chose had the great privilege of receiving greater explanations and insights into what He was proclaiming publicly.[50] Jesus proclaimed that "the words that I speak to you are spirit, and they are life" (John 6:63).

Hearing the Word of God is essential to growing as a Christian and living a life of faith. Paul wrote:

> So then faith comes by hearing, and hearing by the word
> of God.   (Romans 10:17)

Hearing the Word of God comes as a byproduct of a life of fellowship and communion with God. As already mentioned, Jesus taught us that every citizen of the kingdom has the ability to hear and know the voice of God.

We also hear the Word of God in the teaching, preaching, and proclamations of the Word through the gifts Jesus has given to the church. One of the fruits of Jesus' victory over hell, death, and the grave was that He gave gifts to men. The gifts He gave to people were the offices of apostle, prophet, evangelist, pastor, and teacher. During His earthly ministry, Jesus functioned in all five of these ministry offices. They are now given to the church as gifts operating through divinely chosen men and women to equip the saints for the work of the

---

48.   See 1 Corinthians 13:2.
49.   See Matthew 4:23; Matthew 5:1; Luke 10:38-42.
50.   See Matthew 13:11.

ministry. If we are being properly taught and equipped for the work of the ministry, then we have the opportunity to become a person who is strong in faith.

God's desire is that our teaching and training take place within the context of community. We are invited to a diverse community known as the church to continually hear the Word of God. As we continually hear the Word, faith should rise within us and grow us into maturity.

The gathered community known as the church has many diverse expressions. It can be thousands of kingdom citizens gathering together on Sunday morning or just a handful of people meeting in a home. The desire of God is to connect us with a particular expression of other believers chosen by God Himself. God builds His body through the community He has birthed. The community to which we should connect is chosen by God and crucial to the development of our life of faith.

OBEDIENCE

A posture of surrender unlocks our heart to hear the Word of God. When we hear the Word of God, we must be intentional to receive it. When we receive it, God's desire is that we would obey quickly. Often, our obedience to the Word requires us to move in ways we would never have considered or thought possible. Yet, this is one of God's great desires for our lives: Our belief in God can cause us to do the impossible.[51] Because of our trust in God, He wants to see the impossible displayed through our lives on a routine basis.

A critical aspect of the disciples' training was the juncture when Jesus released them to replicate His ministry. The physician Luke recorded this: Then He called His twelve disciples together and gave them power and authority over all demons, and to cure diseases. He sent them to preach the kingdom of God and to heal the sick. And He said to them, "Take nothing for the journey, neither staffs nor bag nor bread nor money; and do not have two tunics apiece" (Luke 9:1-3). The only qualifications and experience the disciples had for this mission was the calling they had from the Father and Jesus' word to them

---

51.   See Mark 9:23.

that authorized them to go! It was a beautiful walk of faith in every way, as Jesus specifically commanded them not to bring a supply of food or money.

Yet, as these weak, flawed men obeyed God, they reproduced and multiplied the ministry of Jesus in their generation. The same reality exists today. God's purpose is fulfilled through weak people who have chosen to make the continual choice to simply obey and trust Him. Our trust in God allows us to reproduce the ministry of Jesus on the earth. That all His followers would reproduce Jesus' ministry through their individual assignments is God's cornerstone goal.

Our purpose is given to us by the Father the moment we enter the kingdom of God. Whether or not we choose to live in the fullness of that purpose is determined by our obedience to the Word of God. When we are properly relating to God, He will continually challenge us to obey. It is His continual challenge that often brings deliverance, so that we do not have our affections rooted in the wrong reality. The gospel of Matthew records the following discussion between Jesus and a young man who approached him with a question:

> *Now behold, one came and said to Him, "Good Teacher, what good thing shall I do that I may have eternal life?" So He said to him, "Why do you call Me good? No one is good but One, that is, God. But if you want to enter into life, keep the commandments." He said to Him, "Which ones?" Jesus said, " 'You shall not murder,' 'You shall not commit adultery,' 'You shall not steal,' 'You shall not bear false witness,' 'Honor your father and your mother,' and, 'You shall love your neighbor as yourself.'" The young man said to Him, "All these things I have kept from my youth. What do I still lack?" Jesus said to him, "If you want to be perfect, go, sell what you have and give to the poor, and you will have treasure in heaven; and come, follow Me." But when the young man heard that saying, he went away sorrowful, for he had great possessions.*

> (Matthew 19:16-22)

The young man desired eternity with God. Jesus explained that eternity with God could be received by keeping the commandments. The young man had, in fact, been keeping the commandments, but Jesus knew the young man was asking the question because he knew something was still missing. It's likely that he was quite wealthy because he was being obedient to the commandments. Yet, it seems that in the foundation of his heart, he had begun to love money and wealth over the God who had brought him the blessings in his life. Jesus challenged the young man to surrender what was holding his greatest affection. Jesus' invitation to surrender wealth was also an opportunity for a divine exchange. The young man could have exchanged his wealth for the privilege of walking closely with Jesus. As we walk with the Godhead, there will be continual invitations to surrender anything that compromises the foundation of our heart. If we make the choice to surrender, we are offered the same reality Jesus extended to the young man: to walk with Him more closely. We can count on God to continually challenge us to surrender any area of our heart which holds a greater affection for anything other than Him. It is the will of God to deliver us from trusting in anything else but Him and Him alone.

The journey of obeying God is one of great joy and beauty. Much like this young man, we can be in Christ and obeying God correctly for a large majority of our lives but still have areas which God will confront in order to bring deliverance and freedom. Learning to obey and trust is what brings us into the experience of life and freedom in the kingdom of God.

SEEING AND REMEMBERING

Miracles and supernatural expressions are essential to our development process in the kingdom of God. Miracles and supernatural expressions are essential because they give us visible demonstrations of God's faithfulness. It is only in trusting the words of God and acting on the Word that we come to actually experience that faithfulness. James taught:

> *Thus also faith by itself, if it does not have works, is*
> *dead.* (James 2:17)

The gospel of John records Jesus' first miracle: turning the water into wine. After witnessing the miracle, John records that "His disciples believed in Him" (John 2:11). The disciples had already "forsook all" and followed Jesus, but as they saw and experienced His first miracle, their belief in Him was reaffirmed. When we see and experience God's supernatural intervention, it is vital that we are intentional in allowing what we saw and experienced to reaffirm our belief in God, too. For many years, God has graciously and powerfully poured out His spirit around the world through the ministry He has given me. I have learned to make it a practice to continually take time to give thanks for the faithfulness of God and reaffirm my commitment to, and love for, Him. The psalmist declared, "I will extol You, O Lord, for You have lifted me up" (Psalm 30:1a).

Jesus continually challenged His disciples to become participators in supernatural exploits. As they followed His instructions, they witnessed and experienced the power of God operating through their lives. God delighted in releasing His power through the disciples' hands, but He also desired that their experience would change their perspective.

Faith is the power of God in operation that brings what is outside His will into His will.

One of the purposes of God is releasing us to experience the miraculous and the supernatural and as a result, cause us to think and see reality from God's perspective. Mark's gospel records how Jesus invited the disciples to participate in the miracle of multiplying the five loaves and two fish to feed thousands of people. After this took place, Jesus directed His disciples to get into a boat to cross to the other side while He went to the mountain to pray. While they were in the middle of the water, a great wind impeded their progress. Jesus walked on the sea to them. As He got into the boat with them, the wind ceased.[52]

---

52. See Mark 6:30-51.

The disciples were "greatly amazed in themselves beyond measure" (Mark 6:51). Though the disciples marveled at what had taken place, it is recorded: "For they had not understood about the loaves, because their heart was hardened" (Mark 6:52). Jesus graciously intervened in the disciples' moment of need, but it is clear that a lesson was still to be learned from the miracle they had just experienced.

This lesson was not learned properly because they did not allow the experience to change how they approached the storm that they faced almost immediately after the miracle of multiplication. It is very likely that the will of God was for the disciples to take their God-given authority to speak to the storm themselves. Instead, Jesus rescued them. Jesus had instructed them to go to the other side. God desired that what they saw and experienced in the multiplying of the food would change how they approached the storm too.

> **The earth cannot function as God intended without the Word of God in operation.**

God releases miracles and supernatural displays to teach us how to see reality. Testimonies not only tell the story of what God has done, but they also tell about the nature of God and His desire to do those exploits again. The psalmist declared, "Blessed are those who keep His testimonies, who seek Him with the whole heart!" (Psalm 119:2). When we see or experience a miracle of financial provision, it should cause us to see any financial challenge or difficulty through the lens of what we have experienced in God. When we see or experience a sign and wonder in a physical body, it should cause us to view any sickness or disease through that lens. When we see or experience someone who is tormented in their mind to be completely delivered and brought into freedom, it should cause us to see all who are tormented and oppressed through that lens in the future. When we see the most hardened person surrender their life to God, it should cause us to see all unsaved people through the lens of what we have seen God do through that experience.

Jesus declared to His disciples: "Blessed are the eyes which see the things you see" (Luke 10:23). There is power and blessing released to us when we see and experience God's miraculous displays. We should never make a formula in the method of intervention, but at the same time, we must remember that what we experience is given to us as a gift and a reminder of God's faithfulness. God intends that His people would interpret everything they experience on earth through the lens of His goodness and faithfulness. Learning to see reality through that lens is an essential foundational piece to growing in a life of faith.

Key Concepts from Chapter 4

- Everything God requires of humanity He first gives as a gift.

- All of humanity is building their life in a certain manner.

- Every citizen of the kingdom must develop and grow in a life of faith.

- Fellowship and intimacy with God is essential to growing in Him.

- Hearing the Word of God is essential to abiding in Jesus and walking in faith.

- Connecting to a community of believers is essential to living a life of faith.

- Acting on the Word of God and seeing the miraculous is vital to our growth and the strength of our faith.

CHAPTER 5

You Can Have
What You Say

"For assuredly, I say to you, whoever says to this mountain, 'Be
removed and be cast into the sea,' and does not doubt in his heart,
but believes that those things he says will be done, he will have
whatever he says."
(Mark 11:23)

April 6, 2020
Words from Heaven

I CREATED THE WORLD *with words because they expressed My in-*
tent. Today, I give words to My people to release My divine intent
and purpose for their lives and the world. This is a season in which I
am releasing unprecedented power and life on the words My people
speak. Do not grow weary in well doing; do not listen to the enemy
as he tries to convince you that the words you speak are ineffective.
Do not exchange words with him. I tell you, this will be a season of
declaring and seeing at an accelerated pace as never before.

This is a season of the word of the Lord coming to completion, but
My people must maintain a childlike heart and a posture of fellow-
ship and listening. This generation will see what previous generations
never saw or thought were possible. The fire of God will be released
through the word of the Lord on My people's lips as they declare and
bring the earth into alignment as I desire it to be. Be sure that you are

releasing My will when you speak My words. Know and believe that the words I give you to speak carry power. Know and believe that you will speak to mountains and they will obey you. In this season, I will train a generation of My people to receive and declare My words as never before. Know this: My angels stand at attention to go forth on behalf of My purpose to fulfill My words coming out of My people's mouths in this season.

God has faith, and humanity can have God's faith. God's faith was created to operate through our intentional choice to surrender. In Scripture, we find a model for the manner in which God operates in faith. A model is a "standard or example for imitation and comparision."[53] We will now look at the anatomy and characteristics of God's faith, as well as how believers can see and shape their world according to the will of God by following God's model of operating in faith. As we look at God's faith in operation, particular attention will be placed on His faith in operation at creation and on Jesus' teaching on the subject of faith in Mark's gospel.

GOD'S FAITH RELEASES HIS WILL

People receive and release God's will through the gift of God's faith. Faith and the will of God are inextricably linked. God uses the power of faith as the vehicle to implement His divine design for the earth. Faith is the power of God in operation that brings what is *outside* His will *into* His will. At creation, the earth was put in order through the power of God's faith.[54] After the shift that took place in the garden, mankind was born *outside* the will of God. The passion and will of God was for all of humanity to come once more into proper relationship with Him. Faith is the gift God gives people, so that they would not remain as they are, but be born-again and restored to Him. The faith of God operating in man is the foundation that changes reality so it reflects what God had always intended.[55]

---

53. "Model," Dictionary.com (Dictionary.com), accessed May 21, 2020, https://www.dictionary.com/browse/model).

54. See Genesis 1:1-3.

55. See John 3:5; 1 Timothy 2:4.

We have been given the faith of God to change the world in which we live, according to His design. Jesus, utilizing God's faith, caused the fig tree to change from the inside out because it was the will of God.[56] As God's ambassadors, we have been given the gift of God's faith so we can shape the world according to His will. Faith pleases God because it is the door to establishing His will for humanity and the earth that He gave us as a gift.

GOD'S FAITH FUNCTIONS IN PEOPLE ACCORDING TO HIS BELIEF SYSTEM

God's faith operating in humanity functions according to the Word of God. He had very specific intentions when He created the heavens and the earth. Additionally, He had intimate knowledge of each individual before the foundation of the world. Created in His image, not only were we to be bearers of His image and carriers of His glory, but we were supposed to extend His glory in creation.[57] God's thoughts and intentions formed His belief system, and His belief system was the basis of His faith. God's faith creates. Through His faith, God releases that which does not exist to be made manifest. God created the world through the power of faith. The writer of Hebrews described faith as "the substance of things hoped for, the evidence of things not seen" (Hebrews 11:1). Faith was the substance that birthed God's desire for the earth. What God *believed* was created through the power of faith that He had in His own power and attributes. God's faith was expressed through what He created. He created the earth through the power of His words which were the expression of what He believed and desired.

Mankind was created in the image of God and was to have their belief system framed by the word of God. God's words to Adam at creation were supposed to shape his existence and purpose on the earth. The earth cannot function as God intended without the word of God in operation. The Apostle Paul declared: "For by Him all things were created" (Colossians 1:16). The Word of God is the foundation

---

56. See Mark 11:21.
57. See Genesis 1:26; Psalm 139:17-18; Psalm 19:1; Psalm 148; Romans 1:20; Ephesians 1:4-5.

by which our faith *in* God and the faith *of* God functions within us. Today, the Word of God comes to man through the closed canon of Scripture and the voice of God which has been given as gift to every citizen of the kingdom. God's voice never goes beyond that which He made known in His Word, so it always agrees with the written Word.

GOD'S FAITH CALLS INTO BEING THAT WHICH DOES NOT EXIST

God's faith in humanity is intended to call into being that which does not exist. In chapter one, we saw that at creation God placed the world into His divine order through the words He spoke. It was God Himself *through the power of His words* calling "things which do not exist as though they did" (Romans 4:17). In this verse, God did the same thing in regards to Abraham having a child as He did at creation. In both instances, God operated in faith: God's faith.

The concept that God calls things into existence that do not exist is vital to our understanding of the nature of God and the world which He chose to create. Through the power of faith, God caused the world to come into the order He intended. Humanity, by placing our faith in God's Word, can also call things which do not exist into existence according to the will of God.

Faith, when operating in cooperation with the will of God, has the power to overcome death. In the gospels, we find a truly fascinating story that illustrates the power of faith as it calls into existence that which does not exist. Jairus, a ruler of a synagogue, came to Jesus and asked him to lay His hands on his daughter because she was near death. As Jesus went with Jairus to do that, a very sick woman reached out and touched Jesus and received a miracle in her body. Jesus was still speaking to this woman when people came from Jairus' house to inform him that his daughter has died. As Jesus heard this report, His simple response to Jairus was, "Do not be afraid; only believe" (Mark 5:36). Despite the mourners and their ridicule, Jesus went to Jairus' house, allowing only His inner circle of Peter, James, and John to come with Him into the room where the young girl had already been pronounced dead. Jesus took the child by the hand and spoke these simple words: "Little girl, I say to you, arise." Those few words caused the little girl who was dead to come alive. Jesus, operating as the Son of Man, spoke words that brought life into a child that was dead.

Similarly, God's faith, operating through humanity, has the power to change the timing of God's purposes on the earth. In His first recorded miracle documented in the gospel of John, Jesus, His disciples, and his mother, Mary, are all attending a wedding. Mary reports to Jesus that they have run out of wine, and Jesus responds "Woman, what does your concern have to do with Me? My hour has not yet come" (John 2:4). One of the cornerstones of Jesus' life and ministry was that He was committed to the will and the correct timing of the Father's mission for Him. The phrase, "My time has not yet come," or similar words occur five times in John.[58] Later, the fact that His time *had come* is mentioned three times.[59] [60] Jesus only spoke the words given to Him by the Father; therefore, the words He spoke to His mother were also given by His Father.

Despite Jesus' initial response, Mary says to the servants, "Whatever He says to you, do it" (John 2:5). Mary had a sure promise from God about the mission and purpose of her firstborn son. Though he had lived a perfect life up to this point, Jesus had yet to manifest all that had been promised to Mary when she was just a young teenage girl. Despite the fact that Jesus declared that this was not His time, Mary's response of faith brought a promise into her day that had been reserved for another day. The next words John records out of Jesus' mouth to the servants were instructions on how the water would be turned into wine. He commanded them to "Fill the waterpots with water" (John 2:7). Later, when the master of the feast tasted the water now turned into wine, he marveled that the bridegroom had "kept the good wine until now!" (John 2:10). Mary's belief in God's promise and her corresponding words of faith changed the timing of Jesus'

---

58. See John 2:4; 7:6,8,30; 8:20.

59. See John 12:23; 13:1; 17:1.

60. E. A. Blum, "John," in J. F. Walvoord and R. B. Zuck, eds., *The Bible Knowledge Commentary: An Exposition of the Scriptures, Volume 2* (Wheaton, IL: Victor Books, 1985) 278.

revelation as the Miracle Worker. Her faith opened the door for the water to be turned into wine; her faith became the foundation to call things that were not into being.

GOD CHOOSES TO MAKE WORDS NECESSARY FOR THE RELEASING OF HIS FAITH

Humanity's faith in God must be expressed through the confession of His Word. God chooses to use words to birth His intentions. Words are also necessary to release God's faith. God's faith does not function without words, much like the human body cannot function without breathing oxygen. One of the beauties of the Godhead's choice to create the world through the power of words is that the Word was God Himself. God Himself was released into the earth to create that which was His original intent.

> *In the beginning was the Word, and the Word was with God, and the Word was God. He was in the beginning with God. All things were made through Him, and without Him nothing was made that was made.* (John 1:1-3)

God's Word created the reality He desired through the power of faith that, using words, called into existence that which did not exist. The unseen realm of God's heart and mind defined what became reality to the natural eye. God's faith is not a life of blind trust but trust in His very own power.

Jesus lived with constant recognition of His deep need for His Father in heaven.

Man's faith in God is not blind trust either. It is trust in a power that will never fail. In fact, God has declared: "For You have magnified Your word above all Your name" (Psalm 138:2). God's Word became a reality because it was spoken. In choosing to create the world with His words, God made the decision to have the world "word-governed." A word-governed world is simply one in which everything that exists is first spoken through the medium of words. At creation, Scripture uses the phrase "God said" at least nine times, expressing that God's will was effectively ordered and obeyed through the words He spoke. Faith was God's power in action to create the universe. His faith framed the world through the release of His words: "The worlds were framed by the Word of God" (Hebrews 11:3). The word "framed" means to "fit or prepare and unite several parts; to fabricate by orderly construction and union of various parts; made; composed; regulated; adjusted."[61] The psalmist declared:

> *For He spoke, and it was done; He commanded, and it*
> *stood fast.* (Psalm 33:9)

Just as God releases His faith through words, humanity was given God's faith so we could speak God's words to release faith. In describing the conversion experience, Paul wrote:

> *For with the heart one believes unto righteousness, **and***
> ***with the mouth confession is made unto salvation.***
> (Romans 10:10, emphasis mine)

Our personal faith in God's Son, Jesus Christ, as the way, the truth, and the life was first believed in our hearts, and then confessed with the words of our mouth. This changed our status in earth and heaven.

God's spoken words framed the world; God's Word spoken by mankind can frame the world in which we live now. The words we choose are the foundation of our existence. Words determine whether we will live in the life and blessing of God or not.

> *Death and life are in the power of the tongue, and those*
> *who love it shall eat its fruit.* (Proverbs 18:21)

Jesus said:

> *"He will have whatever He says."* (Mark 11:23)

---

61. "KJV Dictionary Definition: Frame," AV1611.com, accessed May 21, 2020, https://av1611.com/kjbp/kjv-dictionary/frame.html).

All of humanity will have what it says. It is our choice whether it is life or death. The words out of our mouth will determine if we walk in the will of God.

The words we speak are simply an overflow of what has captured our greatest affections. Jesus taught us:

> *"But the things that come out of a person's mouth come from the heart."* (Matthew 15:18 NIV)

> *The words we release are the result of our belief sytem. Words reflect what we believe, and what we believe becomes the world we will experience. Therefore, we must be diligent, by the grace of God, to guard what enters our heart. Keep your heart with all diligence, for out of it spring the issues of life.* (Proverbs 4:23)

We must also be diligent and intentional to lean into the grace of God to control our tongue. The posture of our heart and our confession should be like this:

> *Set a guard, O Lord, over my mouth; keep watch over the door of my lips.* (Psalm 141:3)

GOD'S FAITH HAS WHAT IT SPEAKS

Humanity's faith in God can also have what it says. Every word that God has ever spoken out of His mouth has been, and will continue to be, fulfilled. When God speaks, it is with an intention and a guarantee that what He desires will come to pass. God is "watching to see that my word is fulfilled" (Jeremiah 1:12 NIV). The prophet Isaiah declared:

> *For as the rain comes down, and the snow from heaven, and do not return there, but water the earth, and make it bring forth and bud, that it may give seed to the sower and bread to the eater, **so shall My Word be that goes forth from My mouth; it shall not return to Me void, but it shall accomplish what I please, and it***

shall prosper in the thing for which I sent it.
(Isaiah 55:10-11, emphasis mine)

The same power and confidence God has when He releases words of faith is the confidence God wants us to have when we release words of faith. We are to speak to the mountain and believe what we are speaking just like God. When we do that, we will have whatever we say. God created His words coming out of our mouths to have what we say!

A number of years ago, I had a profound dream in which God emphasized to me the reality that I could truly "have what I said." In the dream, I was sitting with a group of leaders from around the world in a semi-circle. Jesus approached me and emphatically stated, "Abner, don't you know you can have what you say?" I quickly replied, "Yes, Lord, You know that is the principle You gave me when I started the ministry You gave me. You told me that You would open doors no man could shut around the world for me. You also told me I would go around the world as a minister of the gospel. At that time, I had

God designed us to live with a deep awareness of our need for Him.

very few, if any, doors open to me. You taught me that if I believed what You said and declared Your Word, I would see it come to pass." Though I explained that I knew the principle and was practicing the principle, Jesus did not seem very impressed with my response or my explanation. He approached me a second time and said, "Abner, don't you know you can have what you say?" I thought maybe Jesus had not really understood my response, so I began to explain it to Him again in much the same way as before: "Yes, Lord, You know that is one of the foundational principles that helped birth the ministry You have given me. I have learned to declare what You are saying so we can see it come to pass! Jesus, You have been so faithful to fulfill what You have spoken to me." Once again, Jesus did not seem very impressed with my answer. Finally He came to me a third time. Anytime Jesus has spoken to me, He has never been cruel or mean, but when He spoke this third time in the dream, He was extremely fervent and forceful. It was as though I could see the lightning in His eyes. His words felt like they were pulsating through my body. Once again He asked, "Abner, don't you know you can have what you say?" The dream ended immediately, and I quickly understood the interpretation: While I had learned and practiced this kingdom principle, I had not yet fully grasped the amazing power inherent in the way my words shaped my own reality. Since that dream, I have endeavored to practice this principle more, and continue to see how powerful a gift God has given me through the words I speak. Many times, my current experience has been far different than the declaration of my mouth, but my testimony has been that I can have what I say when I am speaking the words of God—words in step with the will and timing of God.

God has given us His words. When we speak His Word to our mountain, we can have the confidence that we will have what we say, simply because we have spoken God's Word. If the mountain is to become what God desires, it is you and I who must speak God's words! God's spoken Word coming out of our mouth carries God's guarantee of fulfillment. The Godhead cannot speak on our behalf. They have given us words to speak, but the words must come from our mouth. When the Word of God comes out of our mouth, we can have this confidence that we have received that which we have prayed because Jesus promised we will have whatever we say.

GOD'S FAITH STARTS AND COMPLETES THAT WHICH HE DESIRES

God desires to be the Author and the Finisher of humanity's faith. God's faith finished and completed that which He desired. The same faith God used to complete what He desired is the faith we can use to complete His will and intention for our lives. When rooted in faith, our life in God can rest in God's power to complete and bring to pass that which originates in Him. God not only gives us His faith as a gift but He is also the Source and the enabling power of the faith that operates through mankind. He is "the author and finisher of our faith" (Hebrews 12:2). When God operates in faith, it is backed by His power to bring what He desires to completion.

When humanity chooses faith in God, it is backed by His power to manifest what we have set our faith upon. When we choose faith, the power of God immediately begins to move on our behalf, despite the reality that our situation does not change immediately. When Jesus spoke to the fig tree, Peter did not see the change to the tree immediately, yet God's power was already at work. When they returned the next morning, the fig tree had withered from the roots, exactly in line with what Jesus had spoken. Jesus, as the Son of Man, released God's faith and trusted that the words the Father had given Him would accomplish the purpose for which they were spoken. Today we are invited to speak God's Word and rest in the reality that God, as the Author and Finisher of our faith, will bring to pass that which He started.

> **God's goal for every disciple is relational faith.**

Key Concepts from Chapter 5

- Humanity can operate in God's faith.

- God's faith rests upon His unchanging Word.

- God's faith in us has the power to change our reality according to His divine design.

- We must guard our hearts so that our affections are firmly planted in God and the promises in His Word.

- The confession of the Word of God is essential for the operating of God's faith.

- As we confess God's Word, we have the assurance that God will bring to pass that confession.

CHAPTER 6

Jesus:
Our Great Example

*"Most assuredly, I say to you, **he who believes in Me**,
the works that I do he will do also; and greater works
than these he will do, because I go to My Father."*
(John 14:12, emphasis mine)

April 7, 2020
Words from Heaven

WHEN MY SON WALKED *the earth and declared that those who
would believe in Me would not only do the works that He Himself did
but greater works, I fully intended to fulfill My Word. In this season,
My desire is that My body would realize the fulfillment of those words
as never before. Yes, the earth will never be the same through the millions of believers around the globe who choose to believe that what I
have declared in My Word is available to them. Abundance, provision,
and great victory is My people's portion. My people must learn to live
in victory, even as My Son lived in victory over every work of darkness. As My people live from victory, then and only then can a lost
humanity see what I have truly made available for all people.*

*My people's anthem in this season is victory and advancement.
These can only be found in Christ. The world will shake as My people
step into their rightful inheritance in Me. Just as an earthquake shook
the earth at the death of My Son, so I will shake the earth when My*

children come alive to the resurrection power that is inside them. I resurrect people so that nations can be resurrected. I am resurrecting My body so that a representation of My Son will be seen in the nations of the earth. So position yourselves, My children, and allow Me to position you for the greatest shift and change the body of Christ has ever seen. This is a time of reformation; this is a time of change. This is a time in which My body will believe in Me and do not only My works but greater works, so that I might be glorified as never before and My kingdom will advance. This is a season of resurrection and a restoration of the ministry of Jesus in the earth as never before.

The perfect life of faith is defined for humanity in the gospels through the life and ministry of Jesus Christ. Jesus modeled God's divine design for humanity by expressing a lifestyle of faith without any flaw. In modeling this perfect life of faith, Jesus was not exempt from controversy, difficulty, slander, or injustice. The Pharisees accused Jesus of being born in fornication and having a demon.[62] At times, those closest to Him and even His family did not understand His beliefs.[63] Even so, He modeled dominion over the Babylonian system in which He lived. He was not moved by circumstances nor controversy. He was only moved by the voice of His Father. He was empowered by being filled with the Holy Spirit. He fulfilled the Law of Moses and followed the voice of God perfectly, forever changing the course of human history. His power and desire were not birthed out of His own ambition; His primary focus was to simply fufill the task His Father had given Him. He taught us that if we were to follow His example, we would experience persecution just as He did.

> *"Remember the word that I said to you, 'A servant is not greater than his master.' If they persecuted Me, they will also persecute you."*   (John 15:20)

God has given us the ability to live as Jesus lived because we have been given the very same Holy Spirit as a gift. What was given to

---

62.   See John 8:41,48.
63.   See John 7:3-5.

Jesus as the Son of Man has been given to every born-again believer. In the gospel of John, Jesus spoke of this access when He said this about the Holy Spirit:

> *"He will glorify Me, for He will take of what is Mine and declare it to you."* (John 16:14)

It is vital that we receive the inheritance of divine access by placing our faith in the God who has granted us that access. We must believe and receive the access God gives to all born-again citizens of the kingdom of God as a privilege. It is a foundational position in which we need to stand, so we can live a lifestyle of faith. A failure to believe and receive this glorious access is a failure to position ourselves in the authority God wants to grant to all of humanity.

When we recognize our need for Him, we can be intentional in surrendering our will to Him.

God gives all born-again citizens of the kingdom of God the same authority He gave Jesus when He walked the earth.

Jesus, as the model Son, is the One we are commanded to imitate as citizens of the kingdom.[64] Jesus' life on earth serves as a blueprint for every believer. In that blueprint, we find a definitive worldview. Worldview is defined as a particular philosophy of life and conception of the world. Our worldview defines our lifestyle and the quality of life we will live on the earth. Jesus' worldview encompassed a variety of components that worked in synergy to produce a perfect life of faith. To live a lifestyle of faith requires that we embrace the same mindset and resulting values that Jesus embraced with perfect conviction. In the following chapter, we will survey the characteristics and components that defined Jesus' worldview and caused Him to demonstrate and produce the perfect life of faith.

---

64.   See Ephesians 5:1.

JESUS RECOGNIZED HIS DEEP NEED FOR GOD

Jesus came to the earth that He had created, and subjected Himself to this fallen world in order to restore humanity to God's original intent.[65] Jesus was given the assignment of being the greatest Reformer in human history. He was tasked with restoring humanity to God's original intention. Although fully God, He chose to live within the limits set for mankind. In choosing to live as a man, He would be able to forever identify and understand life on earth through humanity's point of view.[66] Jesus had a keen awareness of His specific purpose and mission for His time on earth. When He stood before Pilate, He told him this:

> *"For this cause I was born."*   (John 18:37)

In living with an awareness of His purpose, Jesus also recognizes His need for complete dependence on His Father's guidance and strength to execute that purpose. He lived as God had intended for all people. He lived with constant recognition of His deep need for His Father in heaven.

Jesus stated that "nothing" He did on earth was done in His own strength. All of Jesus' thoughts and actions were under the influence of the Holy Spirit and led by His Father.

> *"Most assuredly, I say to you, the Son can do **nothing** of Himself, but what He sees the Father do; for whatever He does, the Son also does in like manner. For the Father loves the Son, and shows Him all things that He Himself does; and He will show Him greater works than these, that you may marvel."*
> (John 5:19-20, emphasis mine)

Jesus knew His purpose, but His understanding of the Father as the Source and Facilitator of that purpose is what allowed His mission to be completed perfectly. As our example, Jesus intentionally lived by

---

65.   See John 1:1-3.
66. · See Hebrews 4:14-15.

doing nothing of Himself. This models God's divine design for all of us. God designed us to live with a deep awareness of our need for Him.

A common human tendency, that is a direct result of a thought life patterned after the Babylonian system, is to compartmentalize our thinking. We believe we can handle certain areas of life (those we deem minor or insignificant) on our own, and then utilize our faith in God for the areas we recognize that we need His intervention. This type of thinking is most often manifested when our recognition for God is based primarily on our circumstances.

Many years ago, during an extended time of fasting and prayer, I began my day by confessing to God my need for His supernatural strength and guidance. I was confessing my need because I recognized that in my weak physical state, I could not handle that day's activity without His help. As I spoke to Him, I

> **God has joyfully—and patiently— taken the responsibility to help His children learn the practice of daily submission to Him.**

heard the Holy Spirit clearly speak to me: "You need Me *every* day." God wants this to be a life principle. God wanted to teach me that I needed Him each day and in all things. Recognizing my deep need for Him serves as the foundation for placing my faith in Him in all things.

Our awareness of our need for God is also challenged when we have experienced what we judge as a "successful" area in our lives. Perhaps it is as an entrepreneur or salesperson in the marketplace or as a student. This could happen in any area in which our opinion seems to be working well or does not need much changing. It is likely we will need to continue to hold many of the same values that have brought us success in a particular area of our lives, but it is also vitally important as kingdom citizens that we live with an awareness of our need for God in all areas. It is also vital that we submit our opinions and values to God and make sure they line up with His, no matter how acceptable or unacceptable they may be to others.

A key aspect of living with an awareness of our need for God is recognizing God as the Source of all things. At creation, God's intention was to the be the Source of all things for mankind. The assignment God gave Adam and Eve in the garden could only be possible if they saw God as the Source for all things. The moment they stopped seeing God as their Source, they forever changed the course of life on earth. God's intention has never changed. He still desires to be the Source of all things for all of humanity. He desires that we find our greatest pleasure in our daily fellowship with Him. He desires to be the Source of our strength when we rise each morning, He desires to be the Originator of our assignment on earth; He desires to be the Source of our divine health; He desires to be the Source of our finances; He desires to the be the Source of divine favor that we need to live our lives. In all situations and in every area, He delights in being our resource.

A critical aspect of living a lifestyle of faith is being constantly aware of our deep need for God. When our recognition for our need for God is based on our circumstances, we live far below the posture Jesus modeled for His disciples. The end result is a situational faith, not relational faith. God's goal for every disciple is relational faith. Relational faith can only be developed when we live with a constant awareness of our need for God.

In the Sermon on the Mount, Jesus taught that it was the poor in spirit who inherited the kingdom of God.[67] One who is poor is spirit is one who daily recognizes their deep need for God. In the kingdom of God, the life of power that God intended can only be found in recognizing that deep need. In recognizing our need, we are daily declaring that God is our Source for all we will ever need or desire.

JESUS MADE A LIFESTYLE CHOICE TO SUBMIT HIMSELF TO HIS FATHER

Jesus *chose* to live as the Son of Man while on earth. He chose to submit Himself continually to the will of the Father, and He chose to freely give His life on the cross.[68] In choosing to live as a man in right

---

67.   See Matthew 5:3.
68.   See Philippians 2:7.

relationship with God, Jesus lived with the same power Adam and Eve had at creation. It was the power of defining one's future through the gift of choice. Adam and Eve were created perfect in every way and completely dependent upon God. Though made to be dependent, they had to choose to submit themselves daily to the authority of God and the words He spoke to them.

The power of choice is perhaps the greatest power in the earth today. God has made a sovereign choice to allow people to determine if they will partake in His purposes, promises, and divine provision. God can never bring evil, destruction, or disease into the earth because it is not in His nature to release that.

God's intention has always been for humanity to live a heaven-on-earth eternal existence. His desire remains the same, but Adam's and Eve's choice forever altered how that plan is currently unfolding. God's desire is that everyone would come to the saving knowledge of Jesus Christ, but it is each one's individual choice that determines if they will live in that reality.[69] The power of choice still exists for those who are born-again. One must willfully choose to receive aspects of the kingdom God has made available. Our ability to receive what God has made available is defined by our ability to live a lifestyle of faith every day.

Jesus lived with an awareness and an understanding of the power of choice He had been given. Jesus said:

> *"No one has taken it away from Me, but I lay it down on My own initiative. I have authority to lay it down, and I have authority to take it up again. This commandment I received from My Father."* (John 10:18 NASB)

This is perhaps one of the most strikingly beautiful truths about our Savior and elder Brother, Jesus. He freely chose to be part of God's plan for the earth. He chose to live in a fallen world and never sin. He chose twelve men that He knew would all betray Him, except for one, in His moment of greatest need. He knew that although He would

---

69.   See Titus 2:11.

be the perfect expression of the Father's love, He would still be slandered and persecuted, even rejected.

Jesus lived as a man in proper relationship with God, always choosing the will of the Father above His own desires. It is a reality I find almost nearly impossible to believe and understand, based quite obviously upon my admittedly limited understanding and experience. A human being could live His whole life—twenty-four hours a day and seven days week—perfectly in step with the Father's will? Amazing! However, this is the standard which we must not only believe, but it is also the one which we are required to practice as a lifestyle.[70] God takes

God has always intended that the cornerstone of our trust in Him was to be His great love for us.

great pleasure in helping us live according to a standard that for the natural man is completely impossible but with God's empowerment has been made possible.[71] The good news is that this standard is possible because of the sinless life that the Son of Man lived. Adam and Eve failed the human race and forever changed humanity's relationship with God. Jesus' sinless life opened up the possibility for us to live exactly as He lived.[72]

A key to understanding the choice to daily submit to the Father's will is displayed in Jesus' mindset. Although He had a will of His own, Jesus never entertained making a choice outside His Father's direction. Although He had the same options every human being has, He lived as a man without them. Jesus had made a lifestyle decision to make doing His Father's will His greatest delight. Jesus had a mindset that determined His choices. He chose to act only according to the voice of His Father. Jesus' behavior was determined by the voice of His Father, not by His circumstances. He chose to not be moved by public opinion, the advice of His disciples, the pressure from His

---

70. See John 8:31-32.
71. See Luke 18:27.
72. See Romans 5:15.

family, or even the needs of one of His closest friends.[73] Jesus so delighted in doing the Father's will that He compared it with eating food.

> *"My food is to do the will of Him who sent me, and to finish His work."* (John 4:24)

Food is essential for the human body to exist and operate in the earth. Jesus, likening the will of the Father as food, shows that He viewed God's will as essential to His existence, too.

It was only in the Father's will that Jesus could complete the purpose for which He was brought to earth. In the Father, Jesus found not only His purpose for coming, but also the Source of His purpose. A motivating factor for continually doing the will of His Father was His focus on His mission. Jesus was aware that He had to continually choose to submit Himself to the will of the Father, so He could accomplish that purpose. Just before He was betrayed by Judas and arrested, He prayed:

> *"Father, if it is Your will, take this cup away from Me, nevertheless not My will, but Yours, be done."*
> (Luke 22:42)

Jesus was about to face a horrific death for the sin of all people. He would face separation from His Father for the first time, yet His heart was steadfastly focused on choosing the will of the Father over anything else. He made a conscious decision to do this.

Jesus had this mindset every moment He walked on the earth. He was the firstborn of many. All who are in Christ have now been invited into this same place. Paul commanded us:

> *Let this mind be in you which was also in Christ Jesus.*
> (Philippians 2:5)

God invites us to share this mindset because we have the same resources available to us that Jesus had available to Him as the Son

---

73.   See John 7:37-40; Matthew 16:22; Luke 8:19-21; John 11:6.

of Man. Our born-again spirit is perfect and without defect, just like Jesus. We have been given the same Spirit Jesus had when He walked on the earth.[74] We have been commissioned with purpose and authority, just like Jesus.[75] It was Jesus' death and resurrection from the dead that has made it possible for us to act exactly like Him.[76]

An essential element of being Jesus' disciple is learning to have His mindset. Our challenge as believers is that before we were born-again, we already had developed a belief system that we lived and practiced for many years. We have to make a huge shift. It's vital that as citizens of the kingdom of God, we daily recognize that God wants to teach how to think with the mind of Christ.

The goal of the Father, Son, and Holy Spirit is to deliver us from incongruent thinking and bring us into a life of thinking with the mind of Christ. Our thinking defines how we will live.[77] At the center of learning to think like Jesus is learning the daily practice of surrendering our will to the Father's will. This decision to daily surrender our will can only take place as we recognize our need for God. When we recognize our need for Him, we can be intentional in surrendering our will to Him.

This practice of daily surrender is often completely opposed to the mindset we have developed over the years in which we embraced the mindset of the Babylonian system. A common lie that we have often come to believe is that *we* are the source and the masters of our destiny. As masters of our own destiny, we often embrace a "take control of our own lives" mindset, in which we aggressively pursue outcomes in our own image and our own strength. A mindset that is void of daily surrender to God is, at its core, built on a flawed foundation and will always fail.

Therefore, we must relearn our approach to life according to the manner in which God designed. We begin to approach reality from God's perspective through a lifestyle of daily surrender. This lifestyle

---

74. See Romans 8:11.
75. See John 20:22.
76. See Matthew 28:18-20.
77. See Proverbs 23:7.

must be intentional. We can choose daily surrender by approaching life in the same way Jesus did. Here are just a few confessions based on God's word which you can declare over your life each day to bring you into a posture of surrender.

- Father, today I surrender my spirit, soul, and body to You.[78]

- I present myself as a living sacrifice to You.[79]

- My food today is to do Your will.[80]

- I desire to do nothing apart from You.[81]

In the initial stages, living from a posture of surrender may be challenging. We may sometimes feel as though we are even thinking and acting in a illogical manner. In truth, we have lived dysfunctionally for so long that we have come to believe that our dysfunctional thinking and living is normal. Similarly, when we eat food that is not good for us, our body begins to crave that junk food, even though it is unhealthy, and eating it will be detrimental for our future. If we begin to follow a strict diet that is better for our bodies, sticking to it is going to be hard (especially in the beginning). This is because we have developed a lifetime of unhealthy habits. In the same manner, when we begin to think and act in line with the mind of Christ, our soul will seek to deter us from receiving God's design for our lives. The enemy will also try to convince us that daily surrender is somehow unnatural or a weak posture to live from. Be aware that the enemy will seek to keep you from living your greatest life in God, the life of complete surrender, just as he did with Eve in the garden. The most powerful people on the earth are those who have practiced and learned the discipline of daily submission to God. As we learn to practice daily submission, we begin to experience the joy of living the way God designed. We also develop new habits that are exceedingly profitable in navigating our lives in this world.

---

78.   See Luke 22:42.
79.   See Romans 12:1.
80.   See John 4:34.
81.   See John 15:5.

Developing the discipline of submission daily is pivotal to a life-style of faith. A habit is defined as an acquired pattern of behavior that has become almost involuntary as a result of frequent repetition. Please allow me to illustrate this from my own life. From the time I was seven years old until the time I graduated from college at twenty-two, I was an amateur wrestler. I can still fondly remember one of my coaches telling us: "You will wrestle [in a match] exactly like you practice." Practice consisted of constant repetition. Even in my final year of competition, I repeatedly practiced some of the same moves I had practiced as a child. In practice, we were also constantly placed in the same situations and circumstances we might find ourselves in when we were in a competition. The purpose of this repeated practice was to help us learn how to react to a situation without having to consciously think it through each time. The mindset one developed in training was the predominant mindset one would retain when compet-ing in a match. I still had a free will to think and act as I desired, but the mindset I had developed in training now informed my free will.

The goal of the Father is that we would repeatedly choose daily submission to Him. Our choice to think and act in the manner God intended allows us to slowly develop the mind of Christ. As we grow in that development, we begin to think exactly like Jesus, as though we have no other options. Although we still have the power of choice, our mindset begins to be programmed according to God's thought patterns instead of our own. God wants our first thoughts in any situation to line up with His Word. We begin to choose love, joy, peace, patience and kindness as a lifestyle, and we view holy living as the joyous experience God intended it to be.[82] This is the fruit of Christ's mindset and it is this fruit that our Father wants to see in our lives.

God has joyfully—and patiently—taken the responsibility to help His children learn the practice of daily submission to Him. This is wonderful news because we may find ourselves at times still thinking and acting in accordance to the pattern of this world system. We are not on our own. When we miss the mark, and think in a way that does

82. See Galatians 5:22-23.

not conform to the mind of Christ, we have an Advocate, Jesus, who forgives and cleanses us from all unrighteousness.[83]

The recognition of our need for God should cause us to make a lifestyle decision to submit ourselves to the Father's will just as Jesus did. Submission means to yield to the power or authority of another. As a human being, there is a joy and pleasure we experience through living a lifestyle of submission to God. Why? When we submit to Him, we choose to live within the parameters God set when He created us. This choice of obedience and trust produces immediate and lasting joy. The lifestyle of faith that God requires cannot be accomplished without this daily surrender. We, like our elder brother Jesus, must make the daily choice to live with only one option: submission to the Father in all that we are and all that we do.

JESUS LIVED IN A CONSTANT EXPERIENCE OF THE FATHER'S LOVE

A pivotal moment took place in the beginning of Jesus' ministry. The Father, who defined every part of Jesus' life on earth, led Him to be baptized by John the Baptist. As Jesus came up out of water, the Father said:

> *"This is my beloved Son, in whom I am well pleased."*
> (Matthew 3:17)

The voice of the Father loudly and proudly proclaimed His love for the Son. The Father described the Son as "beloved" which means greatly loved. The Father said He took pleasure and delighted in the Son. A key aspect of Jesus' identity on earth was that He would know He was the beloved Son. Jesus knew His identity through the powerful words of His Father. The Father's will for Jesus was that He would know, hear, and experience the Father's love. The Father's love for the Son was unconditional; it was rooted in the Father's nature and Jesus' position as His Son. In the same way, Adam and Eve were loved and completely accepted before they were created. Jesus was loved by the Father even before He was conceived by the Holy Spirit. Though sinless, Jesus' public ministry and distinct purpose was yet to

---

83.   See 1 John 1:9.

begin, but Jesus was affirmed by the Father by virtue of His position and the free choice of His Father in heaven. God the Father freely chose to lavish His love upon the Son.

Jesus not only heard words of affirmation and love, He also made the choice to receive the Father's love by placing His trust in those words. By placing His trust in the Father's love, Jesus was able to relate to His Father properly. God the Father intended that His love toward the Son would provide the context from which Jesus could see His assignment correctly. Every part of His assignment was rooted and grounded in the Father's love and approval. In receiving the Father's love, Jesus choose to view Himself exactly as the Father viewed Him: loved and well pleasing to the Father.

As Jesus placed His trust in the Father's words, the love of God became the defining aspect of His lifestyle. For Jesus, the Father's affection toward Him was not an intellectual idea but a defining reality by which He related to the Father. He lived with a constant awareness and experience of the Father's love toward Him.

> *"The Father loves the Son, and has given all things into His hand."* (John 3:35)

> *"For the Father loves the Son, and shows Him all things that He Himself does."* (John 5:20a)

Jesus lived with a deep conviction rooted in His Father's love toward Him. He lived a lifestyle of faith in His Father because He knew His Father's nature toward Him. This confidence was continually on display as Jesus joyfully embraced difficult and impossible situations.

A person's character defines whether or not you and I can place our confidence in the words they speak. We have been granted access to an eternal kingdom that cannot be shaken and a King who has exalted His Word above His name. Every Word He speaks and every promise He gives can be trusted. We could never trust a God whose character and nature we did not truly understand, but God's character and nature was intended to be trusted by every human being ever created. We can continually know Him through His Word and through our daily experience with Him. Before the foundation of the world, the Godhead had thousands of brilliant thoughts toward us.[84] He delighted in the day we were born and took great pleasure in uniquely creating each one of us. God extended part of Himself in creating us because He made us in His image. Therefore, we have been given to the world as beautiful gifts, worthy to receive His love and wired to His love. God is love. His love is the basis of our existence.

The love God expressed to humanity was never intended to have anything to do with what humanity could do for Him or how well they performed for Him. The love of God was extended to mankind even after they had totally changed the course of world history through a foolish agreement with the devil. The God who is love came looking for Adam and Eve who felt ashamed immediately. For the first time, they began to look inward. Though the earth and the DNA of humanity was corrupted, God still desired that His created beings know they could trust and receive His love. God's love is always present and always extended to us, whether we are walking in obedience or rebellion.

God's love is extended to everyone, regardless of their choice to submit to Him or not. However, it is only when we become born-again that a divine transaction takes place within us through our surrender to God. Because of our placement in Christ, we have been given the free gift of favor, honor, and righteousness. A critical aspect of that gift is that we now make ourselves available to live in an ongoing experience of the Father's inexhaustible love. It is only through the door of submission that we can position ourselves to receive an ongoing experience of God's love.

God has always intended that the cornerstone of our trust in Him was to be His great love for us. In choosing to receive His love, we displace the lie that we are unworthy of love, which we believed through the Babylonian system. In that system, we are often taught (and eventually believe) lies about God and His love. Some of the most common lies are: love can (and must) be earned; we are unworthy to receive love because of our poor choices, or because of the

---

84. See Psalm 139:17-18.

trauma and abuse we have experienced. We sometimes believe we cannot receive God's love because of the state of our relationships with our earthly parents. Perhaps we think we have disqualified ourselves from God's love because of our own injustice toward someone else, or the bitterness we harbor because of injustice done to us. Unexpected circumstances can have profound effects on our minds and hearts. But none of these are true, and all of them can be swept away and healed by God. He yearns to shower all people with His love by bringing them close to Him and transforming their lives.

If we are going to live in His love as a basis for our existence, then, like Jesus, we must make a conscious decision to receive His love. Just like Jesus, we must receive God's unconditional love by faith.

Jesus was not defined by the world in which He lived; instead Jesus defined the world He lived in.

The Father intended that a critical aspect of our development would be receiving the love that He freely chooses to give as a gift to all of humanity.[85] A critical aspect of Jesus' life of faith on earth was knowing and experiencing the Father's love. If knowing and experiencing the Father's love was vital to Jesus' development, it is critical to ours as well. It is impossible to appropriate that which we have not consciously received. It is very much like the gift of salvation: Although it has been made available to everyone, it must be consciously received. We must agree with God and choose Him with our own free will. Jesus displayed God's passion for us before going to the cross when He prayed thus:

> *"I in them, and You in Me; that they may be made perfect in one, and that the world may know that You have sent Me, and have loved them as You have loved Me."*
>
> (John 17:23)

85.   See John 3:16.

We can make a conscious choice to receive His love by confessing the very same confessions Jesus made. A few pages ago, we read these verses. Let's review them again.

> *"The Father loves the Son, and has given all things into His hand."* (John 3:35)

> *"For the Father loves the Son, and shows Him all things that He Himself does; and He will show Him greater works than these, that you may marvel."* (John 5:20)

As we receive His love, we can have absolute confidence that even in our weakness, God's loving kindness is extended to us.

God's great passion is that as we experience His love as a lifestyle, it would cause us to live a life of great faith. A life of great faith is naturally one of great obedience. Jesus' response to the Father's love was choosing to live a life of obedience to His Father. Our response to experiencing the ongoing love of the Father should be the same. As we live in His great love, we, too, should live a life of great obedience. When we experience true love, our response should be love which finds its expression through our trust in God. Jesus said:

> *"That the world may learn that I love the Father and do exactly what my Father has commanded me."* (John 14:31 NIV)

However, at times even our greatest desire to trust God can fall short, sometimes dreadfully short. It is in those moments that we can still be confident that His love is near and welcoming. It is the love of God that draws us into the kingdom, and it is the love of God that teaches us a new way of thinking. It is this continual process that allows us to live a lifestyle of obedience.[86] It is the love of God that covers a multitude of sin when we miss the mark in our thinking and behavior.[87] Our confidence can always rest in His loving nature toward us, not our own performance or good works.

---

86. See Romans 2:4.
87. See 1 Peter 4:8.

If we are to have faith like Jesus, we must know we are loved like Jesus. The same confidence Jesus had in the Father's nature toward Him has been made available to us. We can have this confidence because we are loved in the very same manner in which Jesus was loved.[88] It is from a place of confidence in the Father's love that we can trust His guidance, even when we are in a place of difficulty and uncertainty. The life of faith is not a life of convenience and ease, but rather one of confidence in a Father who is gracious and near, a Father who fights our battles for us as we place our confidence in Him.

JESUS LIVED A LIFESTYLE OF PRAYER AND COMMUNION WITH THE FATHER

From a posture of knowing that He was deeply loved by His Father, Jesus lived a lifestyle of prayer. Jesus knew the Father's love and pleasure toward Him intimately. One of the foundations of Jesus' life on earth was His vibrant prayer and fellowship with His Father in heaven.

One the attributes of God's nature is that *He is one*. God is three distinct persons: the Father, the Son, and the Holy Spirit, but He is still *one* God. In the oneness of God, the Father, Son, and Holy Spirit are completely united with each other. The Trinity never contradicts itself. Jesus as the Son of God and Son of Man came to earth and chose to submit Himself to the Father's direction. In submitting Himself to the Father's direction as the Son of Man, He could be in perfect unity with the Godhead's purpose for the people on earth. Jesus' lifestyle of prayer as the Son of Man enabled Him to connect and submit to that purpose. Jesus prayed that all those who are in Christ would experience and live in this oneness, too. Jesus prayed:

> *"I do not pray for these alone, but also for those who will believe in Me through their word; that they **all may be one**, as You, Father, are in Me, and I in You; that they also may be one in Us, that the world may believe that You sent Me."* (John 17:20-21, emphasis mine)

---

88.   See John 17:23.

Jesus wants us to experience the oneness He experienced with the Father and the Holy Sprit, so we can know the will of God, fulfill our purpose, and live a life of victory over every obstacle of the world system.

In the gospels, we never find the disciples asking Jesus how to cast out demons, raise the dead, or even how to teach and preach the gospel of the kingdom. While these questions are not without merit, they are not questions posed by the disciples in the gospels. I find that fascinating. Perhaps they did not ask those questions because the disciples understood the foundation of prayer Jesus modeled to them. If they could learn how to pray like Jesus, they would see the same results as Jesus. After all, they walked with Jesus as He constantly demonstrated the gospel of the kingdom in His teachings and His actions. The physician Luke records the following exchange between Jesus and one of the disciples:

> *Now it came to pass, as He was praying in a certain place, when he ceased, that one of His disciples said to Him, "Lord, teach us to pray, as John also taught his disciples."* (Luke 11:1)

Jesus had just completed yet another time of prayer, and an unnamed disciple asked a question that came to his mind through observation.

By watching Jesus, the disciples knew that His lifestyle of prayer was not mere theory but a way of life. The gospel writers give us specific insight into Jesus' vibrant lifestyle of prayer and communion that He modeled. The following characteristics were modeled by Jesus' prayer life, and give us an understanding into how we can follow His perfect example.

Jesus' prayer life was mandatory and intentional. Jesus only acted in response to the leading of His Father. The Father required an intentional lifestyle of prayer. The purpose for Jesus' ministry on earth could not have been successful without an intentional lifestyle of prayer. Anytime—day or night—that the Father called upon Jesus was a time of intentional prayer and communion. The gospel writers record that Jesus:

- Often slipped away into the wilderness to pray.[89]

- Prayed all night on a mountain.[90]

- Prayed early in the morning.[91]

- Prayed in the garden of Gethsemane just before He was arrested.[92]

- Prayed just before the miracle of the multiplication of five loaves and two fish.[93]

Prayer was solitary. Jesus' times of intentional prayer and communion with the Father were often solitary experiences. "After He had sent the crowds away, He went up on the mountain by Himself to pray, And it happened that while He was praying alone..." (Matthew 14:23; Luke 9:18).

These times of solitary prayer produced an understanding of the will the Father. Luke describes that after Jesus had prayed all night, He chose His disciples. This, perhaps the most important decision of Jesus' public ministry, was made only after a night of prayer. These times of solitary prayer also served as moments in which Jesus reaffirmed His commitment to submit Himself to the will of the Father. Matthew describes Jesus just before He was betrayed by Judas and arrested thus:

> *"O My Father, if it is possible, let this cup pass from Me; nevertheless, not as I will, but as You will."*
>
> (Matthew 26:39)

While corporate times of prayer are biblical and necessary, it is clear from the gospel narrative that solitary times of communion and prayer were the will of God for the perfect Son of God. These moments of

---

89.   See Luke 5:16.
90.   See Luke 6:12.
91.   See Mark 1:35.
92.   See Matthew 26:39.
93.   See Matthew 14:19.

solitary prayer produced the power of public decisions that changed the course of world history.

Prayer was a place of encounter. The fruit of prayer was that Jesus encountered the Holy Spirit and the Father. Jesus experienced an open heaven and was filled with the Holy Spirit in the context of prayer. Luke records this about Jesus' baptism by John the Baptist:

> *When all the people were baptized, it came to pass that Jesus also was baptized; and while He prayed, **the heaven was opened**. And the Holy Spirit descended in bodily form like a dove upon Him, and a voice came from heaven which said, "You are My beloved Son; in You I am well pleased."*
>
> (Luke 3:21-22, emphasis mine)

In this same encounter, the Father affirmed His love for the Son and heaven was opened to Him. Prayer was a meeting place between the Father and Son that released to the Son the necessary grace required for the Son to live out His purpose on the earth.

Jesus learned from the knowledge of God. The fruit of Jesus' prayer life was that He learned knowledge from His Father. Knowledge is defined as a clear perception of that which exists, or of truth or fact.[94] Our knowledge is a pivotal foundation for our worldview. Our worldview determines how we think and behave. All people, regardless of their culture or nationality, place their trust in their knowledge; it defines their behavior.

At creation, God intended that Adam (and therefore, humanity) view the world through two types of knowledge: sensory and revelatory. *Sensory knowledge* is that which is perceived through the realm of the five senses: sight, hearing, touch, smell and taste. Through sensory knowledge, Adam saw that the grass was green, the ocean was blue, and Eve was beautiful. He smelled the flowers, felt the earth beneath his toes, and tasted the sweetness of the fruit God gave him to eat. He heard the birds in the trees, and God's voice in the garden

---

94. "KJV Dictionary Definition: Knowledge," AV1611.com, accessed May 22, 2020, https://av1611.com/kjbp/kjv-dictionary/knowledge.html).

each evening. These elements allowed Adam to perceive the world through God's lens. Sensory knowledge, though God-given and vitally important, was limited. Adam could only discover His purpose through *revelatory knowledge*. Revelation is defined as that which is "revealed; appropriately, the disclosure of truth to men by God Himself."[95] Adam could not discover the reason for His existence through his five senses. Adam's purpose was found outside of himself; he could only find it through his Creator. It was not until God spoke His blessing over Adam and commanded him to have dominion that the world could become as God intended. Words from the heart of God were spoken to Adam and Eve so they could place their trust in God and forever be established in truth.

> *Then God blessed them, and God said to them, "Be fruitful and multiply; fill the earth and subdue it; have dominion over the fish of the sea, over the birds of the air, and over every living thing that moves on the earth."* (Genesis 1:28)

God's desire in creating humanity was to have a people who could trust every word that proceded out of His mouth. The knowledge He gave to His children was to be the Supreme Authority by which they were governed. For eternity, God desired to teach humanity about Himself and how He intended the world to function. What began at creation was simply the beginning of mankind's education. God's desire was to progressively declare revelation knowledge to Adam and the rest of humanity that would cause them to live an eternal and abundant life, producing on the earth a colony of heaven.

Revelatory and sensory knowledge allowed Adam and Eve to perceive the world through God's lens; however, revelatory knowledge superseded sensory knowledge. God placed man and woman in a perfect and beautiful garden which contained the Tree of the Knowledge of Good and Evil. Although the fruit on this particular tree was

---

95. Noah Webster, "Revelation" *1828 American Dictionary of the English Language, original facsimile edition* (Chesapeake, VA: Foundation for American Christian Education, 1968).

beautiful, they were commanded by God (through revelatory knowledge) not to eat the fruit of it. Satan himself came as a snake and began a dialogue with Eve. Instead of heeding the revelation knowledge given to them by God, both Adam and Eve allowed sensory knowledge to supersede their revelation knowledge.

> *So when the woman saw that the tree was good for food,*
> *that it was pleasant to the eyes, and a tree desirable to*
> *make one wise, she took its fruit and ate. She also gave*
> *to her husband with her, and he ate.*   (Genesis 3:6)

When Adam and Eve chose to allow sensory knowledge to supercede their revelation knowledge, that choice eroded the very foundation of the trust relationship God desired for all people. With trust broken, the Babylonian system, which is governed by sensory knowledge, began to compete for humanity's affections.

Jesus, as Savior, overcame in the place where Adam and Eve had failed. At the outset of his public ministry, the devil came in the same manner he came to Eve. The devil appealed to sensory knowledge and a twisted meaning of Scripture once again. It was in this moment that Jesus displayed what God had intended for all humanity. In every temptation satan put before Him, Jesus appropriated His trust in the Word of God as His highest standard. His answers to the devil show that.

> *"It is written, 'Man shall not live by bread alone, but by*
> *every word of God.'"*   (Luke 4:4)

> *"Get behind Me, Satan! For it written, 'You shall wor-*
> *ship the Lord your God, and Him only you shall serve.'"*
>   (Luke 4:8)

> *"It has been said, 'You shall not tempt the Lord your*
> *God.'"*   (Luke 4:12)

The life of perfection Jesus modeled for us was rooted in His ability to choose revelation knowledge to define His very existence and

His course of action. Jesus did not proceed according to the cultural, religious, and political norms of His day. Jesus was not defined by the world in which He lived; instead Jesus defined the world He lived in. Jesus' understanding of the world and His mindset came from the knowledge He received from His Father.

> *"I do nothing of Myself; but as my **Father taught** Me."*
> (John 8:28, emphasis mine)

Jesus, the perfect Son of Man, placed His trust in the knowledge His Father gave Him. Jesus' posture on earth was the same as Adam's: one who needed to learn to think and act correctly. Through His intimacy and union with God, Jesus was educated according to the knowledge of God. As Jesus placed His trust in what He heard and saw the Father do, the impossible took place on a routine basis. Jesus' faith in what the Father taught Him produced what was naturally impossible. In obedience to the Father, water was turned into wine; taxes were paid by money found in a fish; twelve ordinary men turned the world upside down; large groups of people were fed by a couple pieces of bread and a few fish; the deaf heard; the demonized were set free; and the Son of Man rose from the dead on the third day.

Jesus' ability to be governed by revelation knowledge changed the course of history. A life defined by sensory knowledge or one in which choices are seldom made according to revelation knowledge will produce a life lived far below the standards God intended for those who are in Christ. One of the great joys of being a citizen of the kingdom is that God intends that we be educated and fashioned according to a whole new way of living that is in line with the new nature He has given us. Like Jesus, we must maintain a posture of humility displayed by our ability as lifelong learners of the knowledge of God. Jesus, as the perfect Son of Man, was continually learning from His Father in heaven. How much more do we, as people who are far from perfection, need to live as lifelong learners. The world we have been called to transform lives is in a great deficit when we fail to live by faith in the knowledge God so desires to share with His people.

Today, Jesus' life of faith is the invitation given to His body around the world. Will we allow ourselves to be educated according to the revelation knowledge of God? Only this revelation knowledge will allow us to build the church of the Lord Jesus as God intends. Only the revelation knowledge of God will unlock the billion soul harvest God wants to grant to the body of Christ. Only the knowledge of God will unlock the great transfer of wealth He wants to give. Only the knowledge of God will give believers supernatural understanding of mysteries that will, in turn, give them the status they need in their sphere of influence to reach the potential God has purposed for them. Only the knowledge of God gives understanding on how to effectively see the gospel of the kingdom transform the cities, regions, and nations of the earth.

Because of His love for humanity, God has a deep longing to share the secrets of His heart with people so that history will be written according to His purpose. Our ability to hear and place our trust in the knowledge of God will determine whether or not we live out God's purpose for this season in human history.

Jesus' perfect life of faith serves not only as an invitation but as the standard by which God measures His people. The fruit of Jesus' perfect life of faith changed the world forever. Jesus prophesied that it was our inheritance that we do even greater works than He did, if we simply placed our faith in Him.[96] Our responsibility to God and humanity is that we adapt the mindsets and values of the Son of Man so that the fruit of our lives would be the same as His. The heart of God longs to transform the history of the nations of the earth, but His desire can only be fulfilled if His people choose a lifestyle of faith. Will you choose to be one of those who decides to live a lifestyle of faith that pleases God?

---

96.   See John 14:12.

Key Concepts from Chapter 6

- Jesus lived and modeled God's original intent for humanity through His earthly life.

- In modeling what God intended for humanity, Jesus lived the perfect life of faith.

- In our lives, kingdom citizens have access to the same authority Jesus had.

- Having been given the same model, we are commanded to imitate Jesus if we are to live according to God's divine design.

- The perfect life of faith encompasses a variety of components and core values which include: recognizing our deep need for God; knowing, experiencing, and receiving the Father's love; and living a lifestyle of prayer and fellowship with God.

- God wants to shape world history through His body, as we seek to reproduce the lifestyle Jesus modeled in His earthly ministry.

CHAPTER 7

Lessons in Trust from the Life of David

*For David, after he had served his own generation
by the will of God, fell asleep, was buried with
his fathers, and saw corruption.*
(Acts 13:36)

April 3, 2020
Words from Heaven

THERE IS A CALL *from heaven in this season in human history. It is
a call like that which was upon My servant, David. I am indeed going
to find multitudes with the same spirit and the same mind that was
in David. This will be a global people that will shift the very foundation of My church. Yes, an earthquake is being released into My body
worldwide in this season. As this earthquake is released, all that is
not birthed from heaven will leave the foundation of the body and be
replaced with kingdom realities. As it was in the days of David when
Saul was simply My consent to people's desires, I am Myself shifting
timing and seasons in the earth for My people.*

*I am anointing Davids through true prophetic calls that will stand
and lead the people of God as a Davidic people like never before.
These leaders will be both men and women and are ordained for such*

a time as this! They will love the beauty of My face and learn to live from the pleasure of My countenance as their highest desire. As David did, they will build structures that will bring people together to experience My power and presence. My power and My presence will be restored to My local bodies as never before, and unity and teamwork will be birthed among Davidic leaders such as the world has never seen. I am delivering My leaders and My body from the false mindsets and religious and political bondages that have kept them bound. I am coming to earth, says the Lord, with divine justice as never before. I am bringing My people into alignment with Me as never before. From a place of knowing My beauty, My Davidic body will stand in a place of faith as never before. They will not only speak and declare My Word, but they will execute judgment over the Goliaths, the mountains, and the intimidations that have stood in front of the people of God.

The destinies of nations hang in the balance in this season. I am sitting on My throne, watching to see how My people respond in this season. This is not a season in which I desire My people to shrink back, but one for them to lean into heaven and act and move according to the Word of the Lord. I, the Lord, stand ready to back My people up in this season in an unprecedented manner. I, the Lord, am a jealous God—jealous for My name and jealous to see My purposes established among My people, so that the history of the earth could be as I intend it to be.

So I say to My people: Rise up and take the place of authority and power I have given you to see every obstacle and mountain bow down to My name and My power. Just as David conquered and forever ended Goliath's hold on the people of God, I will prosper My people in this season by forever ending the attacks and strongholds certain Goliaths have held over the people of God.

This is a season for the people of God to forever end the hold of the enemy and see My ability to bring victory in the midst of areas in which some in the body of Christ see no path to victory. The Davids must rise up in this hour so that, like David of old, personal victories can become corporate victories for the people of God. I want My people to be instruments of breakthrough and courage in the middle of fear, chaos, and uncertainty. This is a unique time in the history of the world. I will cause those who choose to trust in Me to advance My purposes in the earth and bring great glory to My name.

David, the man after God's own heart, carries a unique place as an ancestor, forerunner, and foreshadower of the Lord Jesus Christ. The New Testament contains fifty-eight references to David, including the oft-repeated title given to Jesus: Son of David. James, the brother of Jesus, declared at the Jerusalem Council that in the last days, God would "rebuild the tabernacle of David" (Acts 15:16a). For this desire to be fulfilled, God needs a New Testament kingdom people who embrace the value system that served as David's strength.

One of David's definitive characteristics was that he was a warrior. A warrior is "a soldier; a man engaged in military life, emphatically, a brave man: a good soldier."[97] God is seeking—and will find—a generation of warriors like David in this season in history. God's great desire is to change the course of our history through a people called by His name. These will be a people who know His ways, love His character and His Word, and who, like David, will stand strong against the Goliaths that stand in opposition to the purposes of God and His people. This people will, like David, continue to declare victory even as a present-day Goliath speaks words of destruction and slander. These people will not be moved by what they see and hear, but through great acts of courage and boldness based on the authority God has given them through His Word, they will take down every ungodly goliath that stands in God's way.

> God needs a New Testament kingdom people who embrace the value system that served as David's strength.

---

97. KJV Dictionary Definition: Warrior," AV1611.com, accessed May 22, 2020, https://av1611.com/kjbp/kjv-dictionary/warrior.html)

In the following chapter, we will look at two foundational stories from the life of David: His anointing as king of Israel by the prophet Samuel and his defeat of the giant Goliath. As we survey these two unique narratives, we will highlight valuable lessons that can be gleaned from them. If we learn and apply them, they will help us live a lifestyle of faith.

Our introduction to David begins with God speaking to one of the greatest prophets that ever lived: Samuel. Samuel's prophetic ministry was such that "God let none of His words fall to the ground" (1 Samuel 3:19). Samuel, though connected to an inferior covenant, had a prophetic ministry that was one hundred percent accurate. God spoke to Samuel about going to the home of Jesse:

> *"For I have provided Myself a king among his sons."*
> (1 Samuel 16:1)

God had uniquely chosen David for a specific time period in history and with a specific purpose: to rule as a godly king. Even as a human being with obvious weaknesses, David's life was an expression of God's specific plan for humanity. God's purposes are always divinely connected to weak people who, through His strength, will submit to His will. Our ability to place our faith in God for His purpose is the avenue through which God's plans for humanity are fulfilled in the earth. What can we learn from this?

> *Lesson #1: God uniquely chose you and me before the foundation of the earth for a specific time period and for a specific purpose.*
>
> *Lesson #2: Faith is the currency that connects us to that purpose.*
>
> *Lesson #3: As called by God, we connect to God's purpose for our lives through daily surrender to His will, purpose, and assignment.*

By the Word of the Lord, the great prophet went to the house of Jesse to anoint the next king of Israel. The journey to Jesse's house was also a walk of faith. If Saul (the current king) heard of it, he would kill Samuel. Nevertheless, Samuel obeyed God. Eliab, Jesse's oldest son, was the first to stand before Samuel and Samuel was immediately convinced that Eliab was the chosen one. He thought: "Surely the Lord's anointed is before Him!" (1 Samuel 16:6), but God had not chosen Eliab and responded thus to Samuel:

> *"Do not look at his appearance or at his physical stat-*
> *ure, because I have refused him."*   (1 Samuel 16:7)

One of God's greatest prophets mistakenly assumed to know the will of God based on Eliab's appearance. In the midst of this act of faith of going to anoint the next king of Israel, Samuel had to continually heed the voice of God, so he could complete his assignment in the house of Jesse perfectly. Only revelation knowledge released through the words of God allowed Samuel to discern and complete this act of faith correctly. What can we glean from this?

> **Lesson #4: The voice of God released through revela-**
> **tion knowledge is essential to living a lifestyle of faith.**

> **Lesson #5: Learning to place our faith in the revelation**
> **knowledge we receive is often essential to seeing the**
> **will of God manifested.**

Jesse called six of his other sons to stand before the prophet, yet none of them was chosen.

> *And Samuel said to Jesse, "Are all the young men*
> *here?" Then he said, "There remains yet the youngest,*
> *and there he is, keeping the sheep."*   (1 Samuel 16:11)

At Samuel's request, Jesse sent for David and he stood before the prophet. Then, David's eternal purpose was revealed to him and the rest of the world.

> *Then Samuel took the horn of oil and anointed him in*
> *the midst of his brothers; and the Spirit of the Lord came*
> *upon David from that day forward.*   (1 Samuel 16:13)

David, the youngest (not the oldest!) of Jesse's sons, had been chosen by God Himself to shape the course of world history.

One of the most stunning aspects of this narrative is that although David's own father did not think to call him to stand before the prophet, God the Father found him and anointed him and appointed him for His purpose. It was the Word of the Lord from God's spokesperson on the earth and the anointing from heaven that established David's purpose. This is an old covenant example and an illustration of our new birth in the kingdom of God. God's kindness draws us into His purpose, no matter how we have been victimized. Even our previous poor choices can be redeemed by our kind Father who works all things according to the counsel of His will for those that love Him.[98] Here's three more ideas we can appropriate:

> **Lesson #6: Our identity permanently changes from victim to overcomer when we become citizens of the kingdom.**
>
> **Lesson #7: God looks for humanity in their weakness to establish them in His purpose.**
>
> **Lesson #8: God intended our lives to be established by His Word and the anointing of the Holy Spirit.**

David was only a teenager when He was called and anointed to be the next king of Israel. David's purpose and assignment went far beyond anything he could have ever conceived in his own mind and intellect. God created humanity with the unique ability that as they placed their faith in Him, He would cause them to dream and manifest a life far beyond what they ever imagined on their own. Paul described God's plan for humanity in this manner:

> *Now to Him who is able to do exceedingly abundantly above all that we ask or think.* (Ephesians 3:20)

God never intended for people to accomplish their purpose through their own strength and talents. God's gift of faith allows us to trust

---

98.   See Romans 8:28.

Him and express a life far beyond our wildest imaginations. David would need a lifestyle of faith if he were to ascend the throne according to God's purpose for His life.

God's purpose in David's life (and David's faith in God as the Source of that purpose) were essential to David ascending the throne. David was still just a teenage boy when he came in from tending his sheep to stand before Samuel. Even after this life-changing transaction, David's circumstances did not immediately change; it would be at least fifteen years before he even began to reign as king of Hebron. In his own strength and talents, David would never be able to fulfill what God intended for him. It was only God, who does exceedingly abundantly above all that we could ask or think, who could fulfill David's divine purpose. Here's two more lessons:

> **Lesson #9: God desires to give us assignments that are beyond our natural comprehension.**

> **Lesson #10: God's gift of faith is given to live and express a life that surpasses our wildest imaginations.**

Shortly after David was anointed the next king of Israel, the nation found itself in a crisis. The Israelites gathered to fight the Philistines in the Valley of Elah. A champion Philistine warrior named Goliath had suggested a bold idea. He demanded that only two combatants should do battle and winner take all. He would be the Philistines' representative and that the nation of Israel should choose a representative to fight him. The winner would be declared victor. Goliath was a literal giant of man. He began to verbally defy the nation of Israel, intimidating them and accusing them:

> *"Why have you come out to line up for battle? Am I not a Philistine, and you the servants of Saul? Choose a man for yourselves, and let him come down to me...I defy the armies of Israel this day; give me a man, that we may fight together."* (1 Samuel 17:8,10)

Goliath's intimidation was very effective. When Saul and the nation of Israel heard these words, "they were dismayed and greatly afraid" (1 Samuel 17:11).

Through his size, reputation, and verbal assaults, Goliath had paralyzed God's covenant people completely. The Israelites believed his words. When they compared his size and reputation to their own, they lost all courage to believe God's Word to them. They chose to believe what they saw with their eyes instead of the Word of God. God had given them a promise of victory, but it seemed to melt from their hearts as they gazed at this huge man in front of them.

> *The Lord will cause your enemies who rise against you*
> *to be defeated before your face; they shall come against*
> *you one way and flee before you seven ways.*
> (Deuteronomy 28:7)

Even though they were God's covenant people with a sure promise of victory, they chose to believe what they saw and heard from Goliath instead. God's promise was not able to be realized because they chose to believe Goliath's lies. And Goliath continued this unrelenting attack week after week because of its effectiveness against them.

> *And the Philistine drew near and presented himself forty*
> *days, morning and evening.*   (1 Samuel 17:16)

The children of Israel were not bound by Goliath. Goliath was the source of their unbelief. They were bound by their inability to trust God. What can we learn from this?

> **Lesson #11: God's promises of victory can be made of**
> **no effect when we believe the lies of the enemy.**
>
> **Lesson #12: The enemy will often attempt to use our**
> **sensory knowledge (the realm of the five senses: sight,**
> **hearing, touch, smell, and taste) to deter us from be-**
> **lieving God's promises.**

In the middle of this crisis, Jesse asked David to take food to his brothers who were on the frontlines of this standoff between the two nations. David, though anointed to be the next king, had been faithfully serving in Saul's palace and also took care of his father's sheep. David quickly obeyed his father who did not believe that David could be king. David left early the next morning for the task to take the food.

Lesson #13: A cornerstone of the lifestyle of faith is quick obedience.

When David arrived at the frontlines of this confrontation between the two nations, he was just in time to hear one of Goliath's rants. He was taunting Saul and his army, and everyone was afraid. These men, however, knew something David did not know. King Saul had proposed a reward for the man brave enough to battle and defeat Goliath:

> *"And it shall be that the man who kills him [Goliath] the king will enrich with great riches, will give him his daughter, and give his father's house exemption from taxes in Israel."* (1 Samuel 17:25b, addition mine)

David heard this promise once, but asked to hear it again. The men repeated what King Saul had said. King Saul's promised reward did not inspire faith or courage in the men of Israel's army, but it's clear that it did inspire David to engage Goliath in battle. A young teenage boy had come to a battlefield in which the future of a nation was going to be decided. His trust in the faithfulness of God was about to shape the course of history and add to God's purpose for his life at the same time. Never discount the youth because:

Lesson #14: World-changing faith in God has no age restriction.

As David heard about the reward for the man who defeated Goliath, he checked its veracity. He asked about it twice. David began to have a prophetic vision for what would take place when Goliath was defeated. Though the odds were stacked incredibly high against him,

David's faith never wavered, despite the apparent impossibility of the task before him. David was sure that God's Word would be the final authority. David's faith in God would dictate what would occur.

> **Lesson #15: Prophetic vision for the future is essential for living in victory.**
>
> **Lesson #16: We can trust God's Word to give us the prophetic vision that can reshape our world.**
>
> **Lesson #17: God has given us, His children, the gift of faith to dictate our circumstances.**

As David began to have prophetic vision for the outcome of a defeated Goliath, David's older brother saw what was taking place. Instead of encouraging David in this faith endeavor, Eliab became angry.

> *"Why did you come down here? And with whom have you left those few sheep in the wilderness? I know your pride and the insolence of your heart, for you have come down to see the battle."* (1 Samuel 17:28)

David was in the initial stages of beginning to believe that God would defeat Goliath through him, and his own brother questioned his motives and tried to diminish his standing, calling him an irresponsible teenage boy who should have been taking care of his sheep but had left them behind. Not only did Eliab suppose that David was not walking in obedience to what he was supposed be doing, he also judged David by saying he could see the "pride and insolence" of his heart! Eliab sought to define David by His current standing and not by God's ability operating through him. Through his words, Eliab sought to diminish David's standing in much the same way Goliath had paralyzed the entire Israeli army. The enemy used the same tactics of intimidation through both Goliath and Eliab.

In a moment when David should have been encouraged by those closest to him, he was attacked instead and not just by anyone. His own brother, a member of his family, attacked his identity. David, of course, was not just a young teenage boy who should have been tending his sheep. He had been anointed the next king of Israel. Eliab knew that this had happened; he was there. David also has the same right to be at that battlefield as his brother had. David came to the battlefield out of direct obedience to his father. Fortunately for David and the nation of Israel's sake, David was not deterred. He was mindful that faith in God always had a cause.

> *And David said "What have I done now? Is there not a*
> *cause?"* (1 Samuel 17:29)

Lesson #18: When faith is conceived in our hearts, the enemy will seek to abort our faith through words of intimidation that define us according to our current standing and natural abilities.

Lesson #19: The enemy will use people (sometimes those closest to us or even other believers) to release these words of intimidation and limitation.

David's words were noted and reported to King Saul:

> *Now when the words which David spoke were heard,*
> *they reported them to Saul; and he sent for him.*
> (1 Samuel 17:31)

David met with Saul and made a bold commitment and declaration that he would engage Goliath in combat.

> *Then David said to Saul, "Let no man's heart fail*
> *because of him; your servant will go and fight with this*
> *Philistine."* (1 Samuel 17:32)

David's trust in God has now become a commitment to action. Though King Saul was unconvinced, David began to testify and prophesy about the God he knew intimately:

> *"Your servant used to keep his father's sheep, and*
> *when a lion or a bear came and took a lamb out of the*
> *flock, I went out after it and struck it, and delivered the*

*lamb from its mouth; and when it arose against me,
I caught it by its beard, and struck and killed it. Your
servant has killed both lion and bear; and this
uncircumcised Philistine will be like one of them, seeing
he has defied the armies of the living God." Moreover
David said, "The Lord, who delivered me from the paw
of the lion and from the paw of the bear, He will deliver
me from the hand of this Philistine."*

(1 Samuel 17:34-37)

David's trust in God was not simply blind faith but the ability to re-member that which God had done through him in the past. The God who had been faithful to deliver the lion and the bear into David's hands would be the same God who would cause David to be victori-ous over Goliath. David had clearly maximized his time of serving as a shepherd. Serving as an effective shepherd was a training season used by God to make David the warrior God intended him to be. We need to remember these points. Here they are summed up:

> **Lesson #20: God desires to constantly and consistently train us in a lifestyle of faith in every season of life.**

> **Lesson #21: Our testimonies of God's victory in our lives serve as reminders of God's faithfulness on our behalf.**

> **Lesson #22: Reminding ourselves of God's faithfulness in the past on our behalf is often critical when fighting the fight of faith.**

David also described Goliath as "uncircumcised." David's language was intentional. Circumcision was an outward sign that the nation of Israel was God's covenant people. God had given His covenant people a promise that if they would obey His voice, He would defeat their enemies. Even though this promise was given to *all* of God's covenant people, it was only David who received and believed it in this case. If God's people would simply obey His voice, then He Him-self would defeat their enemies. What a powerful combination: God

Himself defeating our enemies on our behalf, as we obey His voice and place our trust in His promise of victory.

David's bold desire to engage Goliath in battle was birthed from his trust in God's covenant promise to operate on his behalf as he went to battle Goliath. Additionally, David had the promise from the prophet Samuel that he would be the next king of Israel. He had yet to ascend to the throne. David was assured of victory! Goliath's defeat was predetermined. David's faith in God and the promises he had received from Him prior to this time defined what would take place. King Saul finally released David to fight Goliath, saying, "Go, and the Lord be with you!" (1 Samuel 17:37).

> *Lesson #23: Our knowledge of God's Word is essential to a life of faith.*
>
> *Lesson #24: Our faith in God is demonstrated by our behavior.*
>
> *Lesson #25: Our faith in God and His promise assures our victory, regardless of the situation.*

David, though assured of victory, still had to engage in battle. Saul attempted to clothe David with his armor, but David realized that He had no experience using armor: "I cannot walk with these, for I have not tested them" (1 Samuel 17:39). David would fight with weapons he knew. He would fight with five smooth stones and a sling in his hand. Goliath drew near to David, and continued his unrelenting verbal assault:

> *"Am I a dog, that you come to me with sticks?" And the Philistine cursed David by his gods. And the Philistine said to David, "Come to me, and I will give your flesh to the birds of the air and the beasts of the field."*
> (1 Samuel 17:43-44)

Goliath's posture and physical stature had not changed. If David had simply looked at this battle through his natural eyes, he would have concluded that not one characteristic about Goliath had changed. Yet

David was not simply looking at him with his natural eyes; he was seeing his situation through the lens of God's goodness and faithfulness. God can be trusted because He is good and because He is faithful. Throughout this narrative, David began in faith, stood in faith, and in the end he was going to finish in faith. David had unrelenting faith in God's power to operate on his behalf. Without this unrelenting faith, perhaps David would have fallen at the hands of Goliath. What can we see in this?

> *Lesson #26: Choosing to have unrelenting faith is essential in living a lifestyle of faith.*
>
> *Lesson #27: In the moment before your greatest victory, the enemy will seek to convince you that your faith is not working.*

David demonstrated his unrelenting faith through the words of his mouth:

> *"You come to me with sword, with a spear, and with a javelin. But I come to you in the name of the Lord of hosts, the God of the armies of Israel, whom you have defied. This day the Lord will deliver you into my hand, and I will strike you and take your head from you. And this day I will give the carcasses of the camp of the Philistines to the birds of the air and the wild beasts of the earth, that all the earth may know that there is a God in Israel. Then all this assembly shall know that the Lord does not save with a sword and spear; for the battle is the Lord's, and He will give you into our hands."*
>
> (1 Samuel 17:45-47)

David's words gave language to his heart of faith. David's words of faith became the reality which he experienced. David did not deny the reality he was facing, but chose to face it through God's faithfulness operating on his behalf.

> *Lesson #28: The words we speak demonstrate what we believe.*

Lesson #29: The words we speak will become our reality.

Lesson #30: A lifestyle of faith does not deny reality but sees it through the lens of God's faithfulness.

David's faith in God brought God's intervention into a seemingly impossible situation. David drew near to Goliath. He slung one stone at Goliath, striking him in the forehead.

> *Then David put his hand in his bag and took out a stone; and he slung it and struck the Philistine in his forehead, so that the stone sank into his forehead, and he fell on his face to the earth. So David prevailed over the Philistine with a sling and a stone, and struck the Philistine and killed him.* (1 Samuel 17:49-50)

A stone, fueled by God's power, felled the champion Goliath. God chose to place His power in a stone that was slung by a young teenage boy who had unrelenting faith in God to bring him victory. David runs to Goliath and kills him, cutting off his head with very same sword Goliath wanted to destroy him with. What can we learn from this?

Lesson #31: The manifestation of God's promise is a combination of faith in God and courageous action.

Lesson #32: Our faith in God allows us to act in boldness despite the apparent impossibility of any situation.

David's personal victory became a corporate victory for his whole nation. The entirety of Israel's army that had been paralyzed in fear for forty days now had the courage to fight. David's faith in God elevated his nation into the victory God desired. And it is David who is revered and remembered as a great king of Israel even today.

> *And when the Philistines saw that their champion was dead, they fled. Now the men of Israel and Judah arose and shouted, and pursued the Philistines as far as the entrance of the valley and to the gates of Ekron. And the*

*wounded of the Philistines fell along the road to Shaara-
im, even as far as Gath and Ekron. Then the children of
Israel returned from chasing the Philistines, and they
plundered their tents.* (1 Samuel 17:51b-53)

**Lesson #33: Our personal victories should also be
corporate victories for our families, regions, and the
nations of the world.**

David's faith in God led to the victory God had promised. The same
is still true today. God has fully committed the resources of heaven
to His people, and within those resources are promises that assure
us victory. In this time, God is looking for people who will choose
simple trust, so that that the victories He has promised will become
corporate victories: for the body of Christ, our city, our region, and
our nation. History is shaped by those who choose to have their belief
system defined, not by what they see, but by what God has declared
to be true.

This is a crucial time for the body of Christ. The history of nations
hangs in the balance according to the choices God's people will make
in this season.

I want to share a vision I had with you: I saw two angels standing
(they looked like they were standing at attention, ready to receive
their marching orders); then I heard the Lord say to me, "Indeed,
they are standing at attention. They are waiting for the people of God
to capture what I am speaking in this season, for when My people
hear, believe, and declare what I am saying in this season, the earth
will change according to the declaration of My people who have put
My Word in their mouth. (Note that I am referring to what I am saying today, and not what I have said in previous seasons.) My people
must understand, receive, and believe the power I have placed in their
mouths when they speak My Word. I invite My people to come to me
with their whole heart and hear what I am saying, so that the destinies
of the nations could be changed according to My divine perspective."

Key Concepts from Chapter 7

- God calls all people into His purposes—purposes greater than they could ever imagine.

- The voice of God and the Word of God is critical to a life of faith.

- Our purpose and assignment can only be fulfilled through a lifestyle of faith.

- The words we believe determine whether we walk in victory or defeat.

- Our faith in God defines our circumstances.

- Unrelenting faith is needed to overcome Goliaths.

CHAPTER 8

Lessons on a Life of Great Faith: God's Goal for Every Believer

*When Jesus heard it, **He marveled**, and said to those*
who followed, "Assuredly, I say to you, I have not
*found such **great faith**, not even in Israel!"*
(Matthew 8:10, emphasis mine)

April 9, 2020
' Words from Heaven

THERE ARE MOUNTAINS AND Goliaths that have stood in front of
My people for a long time. Some of My people have been stopped by
intimidation and frustration; they did not see a way to victory. Oth-
ers have simply chosen to believe there was no way to have victory
over the mountain. But I say to you that this is a season in which the
same spirit that was upon My servant Caleb is being released and is
available for My people, so they can take land and territory as never
before.

This is a season in which My people will begin to take territory
and even—yes! says the Lord, take land and places in the Spirit that
had been prophesied about and dreamed about but never taken. This

is a time to live in the fulfillment of what I have desired but which has never been. This is a season in the earth in which the corporate man will rise up. My people will be a people of great faith—great faith that overcomes all situations, great faith that defines situations, great faith that does exploits over and over again and which points to My precious Son. Great faith is what I desire to be My people's portion; still, many turn away.

It is My desire for My people to be known as a people of great faith. The greater the faith, the greater the manifestion of My glory! The greater the faith; the greater the awe in the church; the greater the faith, the greater the earth will shake. I desire a shaking of the earth in which My people's faith will shift and change their reality according to My divine intent as never before in human history.

As Adam named the animals and forever defined their nature, I desire that My people's faith in My Word will shape the history of the world as never before. For indeed, there is a call in the Spirit like the call unto Peter for My people to step out of the boat and walk on the water as never before. This is a season in which I am teaching My people to walk by faith and not by sight.

This is the season when what My people believe will be given them. So keep your eyes on Me and always remember that I am trustworthy and faithful. When I speak and call, I back up that which I called you to do. I will back you up, says the Lord. I will back you up, says the Lord. I will back you up!

On the first day of each college course I ever took, I received a syllabus from the professor, almost without fail. I was repeatedly taught to be sure to read that syllabus completely, so I knew what was required of me. A crucial aspect of any syllabus is an outline of the course's objectives. One of God's chief objectives for every citizen of His kingdom is that we develop into people who have "great faith." A person of great faith is one who will be able to maximize the power of God available to them and see difficulties and challenges reshaped according to the power of God that works within them.

Simply by virtue of being in Christ, every citizen of God's kingdom has the possibility of developing into an individual of great faith. However, not every person will choose to become that. Jesus wanted His disciples to become men of great faith, so He often used daily ministry activities to help them see their heart condition. After returning from the mountaintop where He had been transfigured in front of Peter, James, and John, Jesus explained to His disciples that they could not cast demons out of the boy because of their "unbelief" (Matthew 17:20). After Jesus was resurrected from the dead and appeared to His disciples again, He rebuked them because of their "unbelief and hardness of heart" (Mark 16:14). Unbelief can be defined as "the lack of faith and trust in God that challenges His truthfulness and finds expression in disobedience and rebellion."[99]

> Our heart posture before God on earth defines much of what God will release in the earth to our generation.

Even though they were Jesus' disciples, some of them refused to believe the report they heard from others about His resurrection. Even after three years of walking with Jesus, the disciples discovered they were in need of repentance because of their unbelief. It is a startling truth that we can be living righteously, yet still have areas in our heart crippled by hardness and unbelief. We can be active members in a church community who are hearing the Word of God properly taught and see miracles, yet have areas of our heart that are still hard and unbelieving. Unbelief can exist in our hearts, regardless of our external reality or our previous exploits and experiences in God. However, this is not news to God and He has a plan.

Lesson #1: It is only in the context of a lifestyle of walking with Jesus that we can truly discover all the areas of our heart that need adjustment.

---

99.   M. H. Manser, *Dictionary of Bible Themes: The Accessible and Comprehensive Tool for Topical Studies* (London: Martin Manser, 2009).

Lesson #2: God, in His infinite wisdom, allows life situations to take place that offer us the opportunity to discover areas of unbelief that are rooted in our hearts and minds.

Lesson #3: God delights in delivering us from any thinking and its resulting behavior that we have unknowingly acquired as a result of being discipled in the Babylonian system.

The good news of the gospel of the kingdom is that God specializes in working with weak people who are simply committed to the process of growing into a person of "great faith." When Jesus described those closest to Him as exhibiting unbelief and hardness of heart, He was not being cruel. He was upgrading their ability to produce greater fruitfulness and power by recognizing the heart issues that needed adjustment!

Lesson #4: God wants His power to flow through us as freely and uninterruptedly as it flowed through Jesus.

One of the tragedies of unbelief is that it can actually stop God's power and goodness from operating in the fullness He intends. Our heart posture before God on earth defines much of what God will release in the earth to our generation.

One day, Jesus was speaking in His hometown of Nazareth. Initially, those hearing Him marveled at His teaching. But as they began to reason in their minds, they became offended with Him instead. Their reason (and its subsequent offense) defined their belief system. Mark records that Jesus "couldn't do any miracles among them except to place His hands on a few sick people and heal them" (Mark 6:5, NLT). The issue was not that God was withholding His power. The belief system the people held defined what they received. Despite their unbelief, Jesus still healed a few sick people, but can you imagine what might have been possible if the people's hearts had been full of faith and trust in the Father's ministry through Jesus instead? Their unbelief defined them to such an extent that Jesus "marveled because of their unbelief" (Mark 6:6). The word "marveled" can be also be defined as astonished or amazed. Jesus was amazed at the people's unbelief.

While unbelief can short-circuit the full display of God's power, Jesus once described a centurion as having "great faith" (Matthew 8:10). This gospel narrative is a clear example of God's faith objective for people. The centurion's servant was described to Jesus as "lying at home paralyzed and dreadfully tormented" (Matthew 8:6). The centurion recognized that Jesus could heal and deliver his servant, and came to Jesus asking for help. Jesus kindly agreed to go to his home and heal his servant. The centurion's recognition that Jesus was the Healer was not what made him a person of great faith though. It was his response to Jesus when Jesus said He would come to the centurion's home that is especially memorable.

> *The centurion answered and said, "Lord, I am not worthy that You should come under my roof. But only speak a word, and my servant will be healed."* (Matthew 8:8)

It was these words of faith and what these words recognized that caused Jesus to marvel and describe this man as having "great faith."

Not only does Jesus describe the centurion as having "great faith," but He also goes on to say: "I have not found such great faith, not even in Israel!" (Matthew 8:10).

This statement reveals a startling truth about the nature of God and how He has chosen to respond to those who choose to trust Him. Jesus was the Jewish Messiah. He came as the fulfillment of God's promise to His covenant people. Jesus' primary ministry on the earth was to the Jew first:

> *"I was not sent except to the lost sheep of the house of Israel."* (Matthew 15:24)

When He released His disciples to minister two by two, Jesus gave them specific instructions:

"Do not go into the way of the Gentiles, and do not enter a city of the Samaritans. But go rather to the lost sheep of the house of Israel." (Matthew 10:5-6)

Alhough it's clear that Jesus' primary calling was to the Jews, the will of God joyfully and freely responded to the heart of faith, regardless of people's cultural identity.

Lesson #5: Faith in God is now the defining feature of the new covenant which Jesus introduced for all people, including the Gentiles if they simply responded in faith.

This centurion will always be remembered for his "great faith." His story is a model for God's intention for all humanity. God's desire is that all who surrender to Him would be known as people of great faith. A life of great faith is naturally one of great power. Whenever I read the centurion's story, I am struck by the reality that Jesus, the perfect Son of Man and fully God, actually marveled and stood amazed at a human being's faith. My continual prayer is that I would respond to God like this too. I want Jesus to be astonished at my trust in Him. I believe it would give the Son of God great pleasure to marvel and be astonished at our "great faith" in God. Right now, Jesus is seated at the right hand of God, making intercession for us, and one of His prayers is that we would be people of great faith.

Maturity is not a measure of how long we have been born-again, but how quickly we learn to trust Him in all things.

Lesson #6: Living a life that astonishes Jesus with my great faith is not one of happenstance, but intentionality.

God is incredibly intentional in everything He does. If we want to be like Him, we must also be intentional. In the following section, we will explore the characteristics and values that define all those who live a life of great faith. In our desire to please God, perhaps we too can allow Jesus to be astonished by our great faith.

The centurion was described by Jesus as having "great faith" because He not only honored Jesus' ability and authority to do this miracle, but he also honored the power of Jesus' words. The centurion said that Jesus' word was sufficient to bring about the miracle he desired.

> *The centurion answered and said, "Lord, I am not worthy that You should come under my roof. But only speak a word, and my servant will be healed. For I also am a man under authority, having soldiers under me. And I say to this one, 'Go,' and he goes; and to another, 'Come,' and he comes; and to my servant, 'Do this,' and he does it."*
>
> (Matthew 8:8-9)

Lesson #7: A life of great faith reverences God.

The centurion described himself as "unworthy"; yet, Jesus described him as having "great faith." True humility allows one to receive God's goodness in the context of recognizing our own weakness. One of the signs of false humility is an inability to receive what God wants to give to us. We are children of God and as children of God, we should joyfully desire to receive all that a good Father wants to release to us. The measure by which we honor and reverence God is displayed by our daily recognition of His authority in our lives. If we are properly trusting God, we will trust the words He speaks. The centurion understood that as long as Jesus spoke the word of healing, his servant would be healed. He believed that would be sufficient to bring the miracle he desired. Our honor and reverence for God is directly connected with our understanding of Him. Our lifelong goal should be to come to a greater and greater understanding of who God is, and how He relates to us. The greater my understanding of God, the greater my recognition of my weakness and my need for Him. To know God correctly is to live continually with a deep sense of awe and reverence for Him. The psalmist declared:

What is man that You are mindful of him, and the son of man that you visit him? (Psalm 8:4)

Lesson #8: A life of great faith is one that boldly approaches God for the answer, and retains a heart positioned in humility.

One of the outstanding characteristics of walking by faith and not by sight is this: Believing a truth brings to pass a manifestation of that truth. Despite Jesus' offer to come to his home to heal the servant, the centurion believed Jesus could heal him despite any evidence with his natural eyes. The centurion was firmly convinced that all that needed to happen for his servant to receive deliverance was Jesus' power of creative speech. Jesus simply needed to speak the words. The centurion's belief system defined what took place in his life—and the life of his suffering servant. He did not let the dire circumstance dictate their future.

Lesson #9: Great faith knows that believing is seeing.

Lesson #10: Our ability to become firmly convinced and walk in great faith is predicated on the habit of continually allowing the Word of God and the truth concerning God's faithfulness to define our belief system.

The centurion also modeled the reality that it is "by faith we understand" (Hebrews 11:3). Faith is what causes us to understand our reality *according to God's perspective*. Faith does not deny reality. The soldier did not deny that His servant was "tormented." It's a reality that he reported to Jesus. However, his "great faith" caused Him to understand that Jesus could reshape that reality. The centurion saw it as contrary to the will of God.

Faith should define our understanding, but all too often, believers require understanding first. They want to see and experiences before they will believe. Miracles and supernatural experience are primarily signs for the unbeliever, so they can see the kingdom in operation and surrender to God. God's desire for those in His kingdom is that they be moved by His Word and directed by His heart, not by what they see and experience.

The disciple Thomas will forever be remembered because he did not believe the report from other disciples that they had seen Jesus.

> *The other disciples therefore said to him, "We have seen the Lord." So he said to them, "Unless I see in His hands the print of the nails, and put my finger into the print of the nails, and put my hand into His side, I will not believe."* (John 20:25)

When Jesus appeared to His disciples eight days later, He graciously permitted what Thomas desired:

> *Then He said to Thomas, "Reach your finger here, and look at My hands; and reach your hand here, and put it into My side. Do not be unbelieving, but believing."* (John 20:27)

Like Thomas, God often relates to us through our current state of understanding. Thomas' words evidenced his belief system. I am incredibly thankful for Jesus' forbearance and kindness toward us that never changes. However, we should want to grow from this state into greater faith. Even though we know Jesus will relate to us according to our present understanding, His desire is that we would quickly mature. Maturity is not a measure of how long we have been born-again, but how quickly we learn to trust Him in all things. Trust is the beginning point for believing correctly as a lifestyle. It is those who believe without seeing that are blessed and can be people of great faith! Later, Jesus told Thomas that those who believed without seeing would be blessed.[100]

> **Lesson #11: Our faith, though unseen by the natural eye, will define what we see and experience with our natural eye.**

---

100. See John 20:29.

Great faith is noted by its unrelenting persistence. Persistence is defined as "the quality of continued effort" or "tenacity."[101] A life of persistent faith aggressively pursues the will of God. It refuses to be at the mercy of circumstances, but lives with the conviction that all circumstances must become what the Word of God has promised.

Jesus was once preaching the Word in a home gathering in Capernaum. A crowd quickly gathered to the extent that there was no longer any room in the home. It was so full that even the door was blocked. Four men brought a paralytic so he could be healed. Undeterred by the crowd packed into the front door, they uncovered the roof and let the paralyzed man down into the room in front of Jesus.

These four men refused to allow any obstacle to prevent them from bringing this man to Jesus. Their faith resulted in action, and that action defined their circumstrances. To act in a lifestyle of persistent faith is to refuse to allow your circumstances to dictate what you believe. Like these four men, our belief in what God will do on our behalf will demand that we act in a manner beyond what is customarily acceptable. As they acted in persistent faith, Jesus "saw their faith" (Mark 2:5). After some dialogue with the scribes, Jesus declared to the paralytic,

> *"I say to you, arise, take up your bed, and go to your house." Immediately he arose, took up the bed, and went out in the presence of them all, so that all were amazed and glorified God, saying, "We never saw anything like this!"* (Mark 2:11-12)

As those four men acted according to their persistent faith, a large crowd of people became witnesses to what they had never before seen with their natural eyes. May we become a people who learn to live according to Paul's command to "fight the good fight of faith" (1 Timothy 6:12). In doing so, the world will see acts of God that they had never seen before.

---

101. "Persistence," *Collins Concise English Dictionary* © HarperCollins Publishers in Word Reference.com, accessed May 22, 2020, https://www.wordreference.com/definition/persistence.

Persistence is also vital because there will be multiple occasions when what we have faith to believe for does not come to pass immediately. A delay in what we believe does not mean it is not the will of God or even that we are lacking faith. Walking with God is not like eating at a fast-food restaurant, in which we order food and within a few minutes, we receive what we ordered. On many occasions, the Holy Spirit will tell us things that will happen in the future, but it will be many years, sometimes decades, before it takes place.[102] Many years ago, I was praying. In reality, I was complaining. I was complaining to God that He had given me certain promises, but they had not yet come to pass. This was His response: "Abner, I never waste anyone's time. People often waste my time! If you will simply steward what I have placed in front of you now, I will fulfill all that I told you I would do. I will do My part if you will do your part." We can only learn patience when we practice patience! God is not withholding anything from us. God actually says that He has reserved blessings for us that are above and beyond "all that we ask or think" (Ephesians 3:20). He wants us to steward and manage the life of beauty and blessing He is so passionate about giving us. It is in the waiting that He works deep within us to properly align our motives, our thoughts, and our character in the righteousness Jesus purchased for us. It is only in the waiting that we can, if we choose, develop patience. As James wrote:

Knowing that the testing of your faith produces patience.
(James 1:3)

Lesson #12: A life of great faith is persistent.

Lesson #13: One of the fruits of a lifestyle of great faith is that when we act in faith, others have the privilege of seeing what they have never seen before.

Lesson #14: If we allow God to have His way in the waiting, He will work in the deepest parts of our heart.

---

102. See John 16:13.

Lesson #15: Gaining patience is essential if we are to live a lifestyle of great faith.

God gives us revelation knowledge and His wisdom as a gift. Through wisdom, we know how to apply His revelation knowledge to our lives. The wisdom God gives to humanity is far superior than reason and logic. Reason and logic is of the mind and intellect. The Babylonian system is defined by reason and logic, so the soul is the governing feature of behavior in that system. The soul is therefore elevated to God's place. One of the common expressions of the Babylonian system today is "your truth." However, God is the only Author of real truth and His truth is unrelenting and unchanging. Humanity can seek to create its own truth, but it does so at its own peril. Truth is an area in which mankind is out of its depth on its own.

People who live a life of great faith delight in living by revelation knowledge. They attach an extremely high value on the wisdom of God. Knowing God's wisdom gives us the opportunity to apply His knowledge, which results in His will being done. Supernatural exploits continually flow out of a life governed by revelation and applied wisdom.

Revelation knowledge never goes beyond the canon of Scripture, but is a clear expression of the Word of God in action. When we live by revelation knowledge and God's wisdom, we become the living word to humanity. When we live as living epistles, people are able to understand who God is and what His intentions for them are.

A key aspect of revelation knowledge is the joy of learning the correct action, timing, and season for applying it. God modeled His infinite wisdom in the creation of the world and His continuing actions throughout world history. At the fall of man, He did not immediately send Jesus as the Son of God to redeem humanity. Instead, He waited.

> *But when the fullness of the time had come, God sent forth His Son, born of a woman, born under the law.*
> (Galatians 4:4)

Before the foundation of the world, God knew the grave error humanity was going to make. Jesus chose to come as the sacrifice; yet, He was not released by the Father to come to the earth until the appropriate time and season.

Lesson #16: A life of great faith operates by revelation knowledge.

Lesson #17: God longs to share the same wisdom He has utilized in history to those who position themselves to hear and intentionally apply it in their lives.

Does not wisdom cry out, and understanding lift up her voice? She takes her stand on the top of the high hill, beside the way, where the paths meet. She cries out by the gates, at the entry of the city, at the entrance of the doors. (Proverbs 8:1-3)

God delights in unveiling His wisdom in the context of friendship with Him. Friendship unlocks the door to continuous revelation and wisdom. This is available to all those who will apply it. The wisdom that created the world has been given as a gift to us, so we can continuously display the nature of God in the earth. Heaven comes to earth when we live by revelation knowledge and learn to apply the wisdom of God. God's Word is the source of all wisdom, and the application of that Word is what changes us and the world to be as God intended. Jesus prayed that we would be sanctified by the truth of God's Word.

"Sanctify them by Your truth. Your word is truth." (John 17:17)

We are in deep need for those who will be governed by wisdom and revelation to take action according to their faith. Only people of great faith can be the answer to the problems of the world in this season. God desires to govern our lives by His wisdom. God wants our families governed by His wisdom. He also wants our assignments governed by His wisdom. God also wants His church communities governed by His wisdom. Additionally God wants our neighborhoods, cities, regions, and nations all governed by His wisdom. God longs to shape history through a people governed by the wisdom of the Master Craftsman who created the world.[103]

Lesson #18: The Source of truth wants to shape our world through the truth and integrity of God.

A people of great faith take courageous action. It may appear foolish to minds governed by intellect and reason. Joshua's instructions of wisdom from God were to march around the walled city of Jericho for six straight days, once with all the men of war. On the seventh day, they were to march around seven times and the priests were told to blow trumpets. After the trumpets were blown, the people were to shout! While God had already promised this victory through His Word, it was only after the people did as instructed that the wisdom of God released the victory.[104] Gideon's instructions resulted in dwindling an army of thousands down to three hundred; yet, victory was once again the result.[105] By the Word of Lord, the prophet Elisha instructed Naaman, the commander of the Syrian army, to wash in the Jordan seven times. After some struggle with the instructions, Naaman finally relented, washed, and was miraculously healed.[106] The common denominator in each of these accounts was that man's obedience to God's instructions resulted in the will of God shaping reality. A life of great faith always sees God and His Word as one.

We must live with an enduring conviction to be lifelong learners of God.

Lesson #19: Walking obediently according to God's revelation knowledge directed by His wisdom can change the world.

---

103. See Proverbs 8:30.
104. See Joshua 6:1-5.
105. See Judges 7.
106. See 2 Kings 5:1-19.

There are two primary Greek words which are translated "word" in the New Testament. The first, *logos,* refers to the total inspired Word of God, and to Jesus who is the living *Logos.*[107] *Logos* is used 330 times in the New Testament. Examples of *logos* in the Bible are:

> *In the beginning was the* **Word***, and the* **Word** *was with God, and the* **Word** *was God. He was in the beginning with God.* (John 1:1-2, emphasis mine)

> *Be diligent to present yourself approved to God, a worker who does not need to be ashamed, rightly dividing the* **word** *of truth.* (2 Timothy 2:15, emphasis mine)

The second Greek word that describes Scripture is *rhema.* It refers to a word that is spoken, "an utterance."[108] Examples of a *rhema* word in the Bible are:

> *While Annas and Caiaphas were high priests, the* **word** *of God came to John the son of Zacharias in the wilderness.* (Luke 3:2, emphasis mine)

> *But Simon answered and said to Him, "Master, we have toiled all night and caught nothing; nevertheless at Your word I will let down the net."* (Luke 5:5)

The *logos* and *rhema* words are always in complete alignment with each other. The primary difference between *logos* and *rhema* is that *rhema* is a specific spoken word or words for a specific situation in the Bible. *Rhema* words from the Father defined Jesus' life and ministry here on earth. Even as early as twelve years of age, Jesus stayed behind in Jerusalem, listening and asking questions of the teachers of the Law, long after His family had returned home. Hearing the *rhema*

---

107. James Strong, "3056. Logos," Strong's Greek: 3056. λόγος (logos) -- a word (as embodying an idea), a statement, a speech (Biblehub), accessed May 23, 2020, https://biblehub.com/greek/3056.htm)

108. James Strong, "4487. Rhéma," Strong's Greek: 4487. ῥῆμα (rhéma) -- a word, by impl. a matter (Biblehub), accessed May 23, 2020, https://biblehub.com/greek/4487.htm)

word from God led Jesus to choose the Twelve as His original disciples, and then chose three to be what can be described as His inner circle. Hearing from God is the reason Jesus gave for not performing miracles in the same manner in each place where He went.

God is still speaking to His people today. He delights in giving His children *rhema* words. *Rhema* brings life, direction, wisdom, and understanding. The words God gives to His people are most certainly not on the same par as the Bible and never contradict it, but they are still vital in living a life of great faith. *Rhema* from God is the tangible expression of *logos*.

Our life purpose here in God is to be filled with constant *rhema* assignments from heaven. For example, God will divinely call individuals to different nations for both long-term and short-term work through His spoken Word. God will speak to an individual about which college or technical school to attend. He could direct us specifically to the one we should marry. God will speak *rhema* words to a family to adopt a child or buy groceries for a year for a family in financial need.

The book you are now reading is the direct result of a *rhema* word from God. My life has been defined by a constant hearing of the Word and God has given me faith to do what I had never thought possible. To live a life of faith, we must know God and His voice. We cannot know God apart from ongoing words from Him. How we steward and obey what we have heard defines the depth of trust and understanding we will come to know. Jesus told His disciples this:

> *"I still have many things to say to you, but you cannot bear them now."* (John 16:12)

God did not tell us everything we needed to know at one time. He directs us daily through the process of friendship and fellowship with Him.

Lesson #20: The proper use of the Word of God is essential to a life of great faith.

The assignments God wants us to accomplish can only be birthed from hearts positioned to hear and do whatever He asks, no matter how illogical or unreasonable His requests may seem to our intellect. Here is one example from my life that taught me the paramount importance of partnering with God and standing in His Word to see His will and purpose fulfilled.

A number of years ago, the Holy Spirit gave me a very specific assignment. He told me to host an end-of-the-year conference with some nationally known speakers. While a great many details and much wisdom was needed for the conference to come together smoothly and with excellence, the greatest challenge was getting the financial resources necessary for the event. The money just wasn't there. However, I was convinced that we, as a ministry, had an assignment to host this conference. An essential value to walking by faith is knowing that you have a clear direction from God for a specific assignment or situation. It's also knowing you are in the timing and season for pursuing that assignment. At that time, our ministry had never hosted an event of this size nor had we ever hosted an event with such significant costs. When we walk in God's faith, we will be consistently challenged to move beyond our current circumstance or into action that we have never considered.

Lesson #21: A word from God births kingdom action.

I did not have the financial resources needed for this event, but I did have a very clear word from God. The word from God was sufficient in bringing me the financial resources I needed! There were many times in which doubt and unbelief tried to challenge what God had spoken to me, but each time, God kindly reassured me that He would back me up!

Our life should never be governed by our good ideas but by God's assignments birthed from His heart instead. An error that some believers sometimes make is assuming that God will do the same thing for them that He did for someone else just because they believe it is a good idea. God has no obligation to back plans He has never proposed for you. For example, just because Pastor Joe purchased a two-million dollar building for one hundred thousand dollars does not mean Pastor John can do the same. God is certainly no respecter of persons, but He is a respecter of assignments and the different journeys He has called each of us to walk.

In the months leading up to this conference, I began nearly every day confessing the Word of God over my situation. I continually used verses like 2 Corinthians 8:9 and Philippians 4:19 as directed by God.

> *For you know the grace of our Lord Jesus Christ, that though He was rich, yet for your sakes He became poor, that you through His poverty might become rich.*
> (2 Corinthians 8:9)

> *And my God shall supply all your need according to His riches in glory by Christ Jesus.*   (Philippians 4:19)

Through confession, I applied the *logos* to my situation. As I did this, my trust in Him was strengthened. The Word of God is the will of God. Jesus promised that He would give us the keys of the kingdom.[109] We know that the will of God is released when God's Word is spoken.

Lesson #22: We are called to stand on the Word of God.

As I walk in fellowship with God, I often seek Him for a specific Scripture that relates to my situation. Very often, God will quicken a specific verse or series of verses to me so I will apply them to my circumstances. Jesus modeled this for us as well. When He spoke, He was not simply speaking arbitrary words. Jesus spoke specific words for specific situations so that the world would become as the Father intended.

> *"For I have not spoken on My own authority; but the Father who sent Me gave Me a command, what I should say and what I should speak."*   (John 12:49)

---

109. See Matthew 16:19.

It is vital not only to know what verses you are standing on, but also to confess them to see the manifestation of God's promise.

One morning about a month before the event, I was spending some time with God. I was confessing the Word of God over the coming event and thanking Him for being the Provider and Financier for it. As I was thanking Him for providing, I heard the Lord say, "You have broken through. You have more than enough for this event." This was a *key word* from Him over my situation. He had quickened it to me. Key words can be defined as a word or a specific group of words that relates to a specific situation. As we walk in fellowship with God, He will often give us *key words* such as this one which He gave me for that event. These *key words* are not on the same level of Scripture by any means, but they complement the sure promises found in God's Word. They are also given to further bring faith and hope to our current situation, serving as confirmations and encouragement along the way.

Later that morning, I called the woman who led prayer and intercession for our ministry and told her what God said. She was very excited. It turned out that God had shared something very similar that morning with her. For the next month, I instructed her to tell our inner circle of intercessors to confess and declare unitedly that we had "broken through" in the area of finances. The idea that we had "broken through" was God's *key words* to us in our situation, so we took our stand on that. God released all we needed for the event and more.

I'd like to highlight one of the reasons it is vital to connect with a community of believers and form covenant relationships. As we come into agreement with people of "like precious faith,"[110] we can "agree on earth concerning anything that they ask, it will be done for them by My Father in heaven" (Matthew 18:19). The agreement over God's *rhema* word between me and these intercessors not only brought forth

---

110. See 2 Peter 1:1.

God's promise, but strengthened and encouraged us all in our faith at the same time. God is continually desiring to teach people His ways.

> *Lesson #23: There is power in agreement to birth the will of God on earth as it is in heaven.*

> *Lesson #24: When God gives us a rhema word, we can stand on that in prayer as long as it agrees with His written logos.*

As we walk with God, we can have the assurance that what He has spoken will take place in the timing He said it would take place, whether or not we see that manifest immediately. We did not receive a check or a series of donations that day or even in the next few weeks that would cover the event financially, but we were believing God. By the time the event was over, though, we received close to $17,000 more than what we asked God for. God always guarantees His Word, and His Word released from our mouth assured that His guarantee would come to pass!

> *Lesson #25: God's Word is a guarantee.*

One of the keys to living a life of great faith is maintaining a childlike heart. A childlike heart has little to do with numerical age, but it has everything to do with the positioning of your heart and the resulting mindset. King Solomon taught us that "the fear of the Lord is the beginning of wisdom" (Proverbs 9:10). The fear of the Lord is simply a posture of your heart, in which God is taken seriously in every area of life.

We must never graduate from living outside the fear of the Lord, if we desire to maintain a childlike heart. Every person in Christ can, without even knowing it, lose the posture of a childlike heart. A common challenge to maintaining a childlike heart is that we often define God by what we have known and experienced in Him. We see God through the lens of our experience and what we know about His Word. He is bigger than both.

Every group or stream in the body of Christ has a certain form that they have adopted and embraced. Many of these are biblically based, but the form itself is simply a method God gave each particular stream. The methods God gives us can be fruitful and effective in operating and ministering to people as God has directed. However, we must be careful to never place *our methods* in the same category or give them the same reverence we give to Scripture itself. Jesus told the Pharisees and scribes this:

> *"And so you cancel the word of God in order to hand down your own tradition."* (Mark 7:13 NLT)

We must never place our traditions over God's Word. We must live with an enduring conviction to be lifelong learners of God. We should live with the clear understanding that no matter how long we have been walking with God, we still know very little. We should live with a firm determination that we need covenant relationships with other believers that will constantly give us feedback and insight to help bring correction in our journey with God. The late Bishop Vernon Ashe once said, "It is only within the context of covenant relationships that I can truly discover what is wrong with me." No leader or parishioner is outside of receiving the correction or insight needed to maximize our journey with God. One of the signs of a heart that is no longer childlike is that a person is unable to receive correction from God or others. If we do not receive correction from others, it is likely we would not receive correction from God Himself.

In Matthew's gospel, Jesus twice expressed the importance of kingdom citizens maintaining a childlike temperament. One day, they brought children to Jesus, asking Him to pray for them. The disciples, unaware of Jesus' will, rebuked them, but Jesus disagreed.

> *But Jesus said, "Let the little children come to Me, and do not forbid them; for of such is the kingdom of heaven."* (Matthew 19:14)

*At that time the disciples came to Jesus, saying, "Who then is greatest in the kingdom of heaven?" Then Jesus called a little child to Him, set him in the midst of them, and said, "Assuredly, I say to you, **unless you are converted and become as little children**, you will by no means enter the kingdom of heaven. Therefore whoever humbles himself as this little child is the greatest in the kingdom of heaven. Whoever receives one little child like this in My name receives Me."*
(Matthew 18:1-5, emphasis mine)

Jesus emphatically taught that entrance to the kingdom only came through conversion. Coversion is not only defined by repentance but also by active believing. True scriptural repentance demands that we change our belief system. If we are to believe as a child, then we must humble ourselves as children. No baby is born by defining the world in which he or she lives through an individual set of values. When born, a baby is defined by its culture, family, and the values placed within that child. We are born-again into the kingdom of God to re-learn the world according to God's value system.

To enter the kingdom, we must repent of everything we know to be true about ourselves and God, and begin to believe as if we were a child who had never been taught. Each of us comes into the kingdom of God with our own experiences, both negative and positive. These experiences will attempt to color the lens through which we relate to God. It is vitally important that we position ourselves in a place of humility before God so the lens of our heart can be continually delivered of these contrary experiences. As Jesse Duplantis fondly states: "God has no grown-ups!"

> *Lesson #26: A life of great faith maintains a childlike heart.*
>
> *Lesson #27: If we embrace our methods over God's Word, we are in certain danger of positioning our hearts in incorrect manner.*
>
> *Lesson #28: We can only enter into the kingdom as a*

*child, and it is vitally important that we remain po-
sitioned as children in our hearts so we can develop
great faith.*

People of great faith will transform the world according to God's divine design. Our adversaries (the devil and his demons) have been completely defeated. However, the enemy is still fighting against the purposes of God through those who serve him and his desires through the Babylonian system. Therefore, God's people who live a life of great faith are guaranteed to face persecution. The good news is that people of great faith have never been stopped, nor will they ever be stopped because of persecution. We need not look for persecution. It is the fruit of living as God intended. Paul, in his letter to his spiritual son Timothy, wrote:

> *Yes, and **all who desire** to live godly in Christ Jesus will
> suffer persecution.*
> > (2 Timothy 3:12, emphasis mine)

Great faith exposes the mediocrity that exists in the people of God. People of great faith also expose the bankrupt and insufficient traditions and evil root systems of a religious spirit. A person can sincerely love God, but still fail to see truth and reality through an accurate lens. The men and women of the body of Christ must either accept God's invitation to believe and live from a place of greater fruitfulness or reject it. Often in their rejection of what God desires, they slander and persecute people of great faith, many times using Scripture and claiming to stand with God as they do so. A common tool of slander is to accuse people who are simply walking by faith of pride and arrogance when, in fact, the real arrogance is in denying the truth about who God is and what His Word has declared to be true! Be vigilant and guarded to never believe the lie that it is arrogant to trust God and His Word.

History does not remember the critic, only the reformer. Jesus lived as the greatest Reformer in human history! He lived and fulfilled the Law of God perfectly. Yet, some of His greatest opposition and

143

persecution came from a segment of the population who claimed to be not only longing for the promised Messiah, but who also considered themselves faithful adherents of the Law of Moses that Jesus taught. However, the traditions of men and the resulting religious spirit had blinded them. Even today, both those things will often enslave and persecute the very thing they claim to desire the most.

It is only through the strength and courage we find in God that we can truly be the people of great faith God desires. A life of great faith is marked by clinging to the core value that it is only the power of God working within us that enables us to live overcoming lives. When we decide in our hearts to choose integrity to God and His Word as a manner of life, regardless of the environment we live in, we are certain to face persecution.

When the decree came in Babylon to worship a golden image or else face being thrown into a furnace, Shadrach, Meschach, and Abednego already knew they only had one option. Even though Nebuchadnezzar had presented a choice, they had already decided that disobedience to God and His Word was not an option. Shadrach, Meshach, and Abednego said to the king,

> *"O Nebuchadnezzar, we have no need to answer you in this matter. If that is the case, our God whom we serve is able to deliver us from the burning fiery furnace, and He will deliver us from your hand, O king. But if not, let it be known to you, O king, that we do not serve your gods, nor will we worship the gold image which you have set up."* (Daniel 3:16-18)

In this season, God will unlock exploits to His people that will cause nations to see and wonder! Just as Shadrach, Meschach, and Abednego chose to obey God and caused a nation to see and know that He is the one true and living God, God's desire today is to give to His people unprecedented favor and advancement as they choose to follow Him, regardless of threatened persecution or danger.

How we treat those who persecute us defines if we truly can be described as a person of great faith. Jesus gave explicit instructions on how to react when we are persecuted:

> *"But I say to you, love your enemies, bless those who curse you, do good to those who hate you, and pray for those who spitefully use you and persecute you."*
>
> (Matthew 5:44)

When we are persecuted, we have the power within us to choose love, blessing, and goodness. When we choose love, blessing, and goodness, it is an opportunity to demonstrate God's posture to humanity. Though humanity thinks and behaves in complete opposition to His love and goodness, these attributes of God are always extended to them anyway, regardless of their behavior. Jesus told us that we were "blessed" when we were "persecuted for righteousness' sake" (Matthew 5:10). We are blessed because we find ourselves in a position in which we can truly demonstrate His nature. In our pursuit of being like Him, all the rest is simply the fruit of a life that follows the Master's footprints.

Lesson #29: A life of great faith will be persecuted.

Lesson #30: The essence of being a person of great faith is not necessarily the great works and abundant fruit we will produce, but rather the call to be like Him.

A life of great faith is not a destination but a continuous journey, during which we are in jeopardy of not attaining to great faith if we ever believe we have arrived. It's a choice to surrender one's mind, will, and emotions to Jesus on a daily basis. When we surrender to Him, we can become like Him; when we become like Him, our goal is just to please Him. When we please Him, we find our greatest pleasure and satisfaction. The satisfaction that we have in knowing that we please Him is something that cannot be found anywhere else in this world. Our reward is not of this world; it is only found in a different place, in which our citizenship is currently found.

But without faith it is impossible to please Him, for he who comes to God must believe that He is, and that He is a rewarder of those who diligently seek Him.

(Hebrews 11:6)

Key Concepts from Chapter 8

- God wants every one of His children to live a life of great faith.

- A lifestyle of consistent fellowship with God helps identify areas in hearts that are positioned in unbelief.

- Unbelief hinders the full release of God's power and presence in our lives.

- A life of great faith intentionally embraces heaven's value system.

- A life of great faith will be persecuted.

- A life of great faith changes reality according to God's perspective.

About the Author

ABNER SUAREZ is the Founder and President of For Such A Time As This, an international ministry devoted to God's scriptural mandate to disciple nations. Abner is a speaker and prophetic voice, advisor, and author. His books and their accompanying guides equip believers to rediscover God's original plan for the earth and humanity's purpose in His plan. The guides help readers dig deeper into the books' ideas without repeating them and provide personal-growth focused discussion points.

Abner's books and guides are intentionally written to expand his God-given vision of building lives established on fellowship with God.

He is an ordained minister with the Apostolic Network of Global Awakening under the leadership of Randy Clark; he holds a Bachelor of Science and Master of Education degree from Campbell University in North Carolina, and a Master of Ministry diploma from the Wagner Leadership Institute. Abner's greatest passion is simply knowing God.

Invite Abner to Speak at Your Next Event

ABNER SUAREZ ministers to a wide variety of audiences within the body of Christ, government, education, and business settings. He leads Encounter Schools, Prophetic Clinics, Discipleship Essentials Weekends, and more. Prayerfully consider hosting him at your church, in your city, or other event. Get in touch with Abner at info@abnersuarez.com or at www.abnersuarez.com

If You're a Fan of This Book, Please Tell Others...

- Post a 5-Star review on Amazon.

- Write about the book on your Facebook, Twitter, Instagram page—any social media you regularly use!

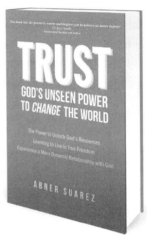

- If you have led the group study or participated in one using this book, share that experience too.

- If you blog, consider referencing the book, your study experiences, or publishing an excerpt from the book with a link to my website. You have my permission to do this as long as you provide proper credit and backlinks.

- Recommend the book to friends. Word-of-mouth is still the most effective form of advertising.

- Purchase additional copies to give as gifts. You can do this by visiting my website: abnersuarez.com

Use This Powerful Teaching on Faith in Your Small Group or Sunday School Class

Order the companion *TRUST Facilitator's Guide* and *Participant's Guide* as resources to lead a small group on faith. The material in these resources are written to compliment the teaching found in this book and encourage dynamic group discussion and interaction.

To order, go to www.abnersuarez.com/smallgroup